Greetings from DALLAS

Mary L. Martin
Dinah Roseberry

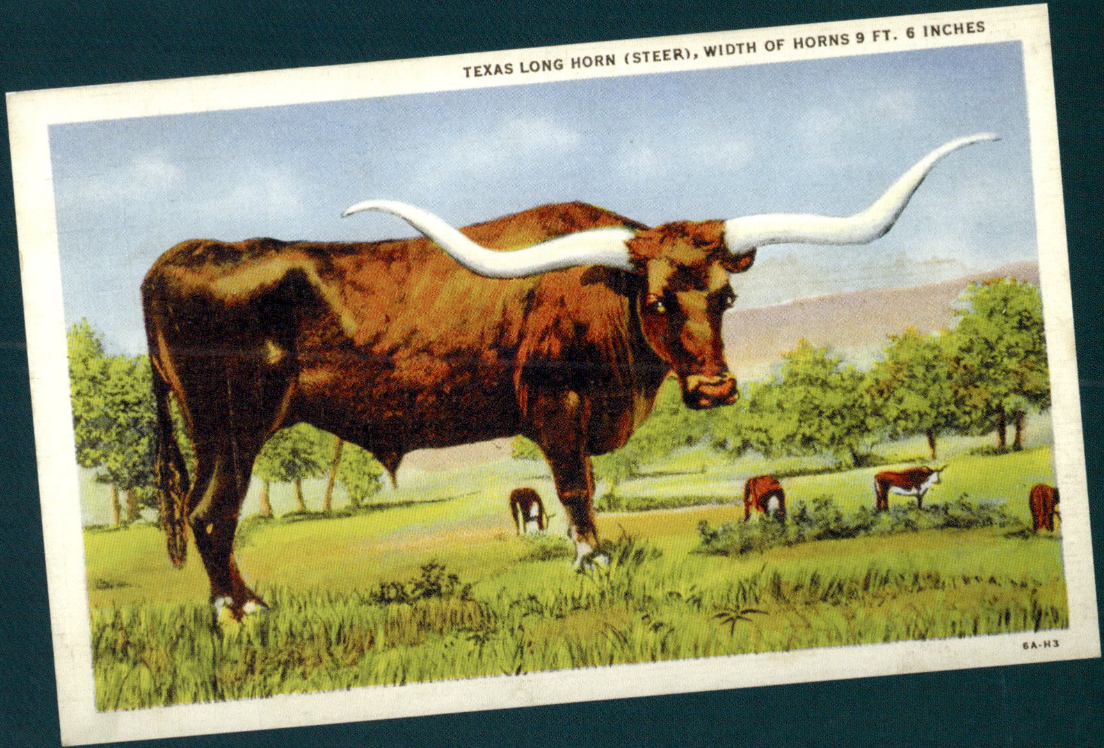

Schiffer Publishing Ltd®
4880 Lower Valley Road Atglen, Pennsylvania 19310

Library of Congress Control Number: 2007936174

Designed by John P. Cheek
Type set in Schneidler Md BT/NewBskvll BT

ISBN: 978-0-7643-2805-3
Printed in China

Published by Schiffer Publishing Ltd.
4880 Lower Valley Road
Atglen, PA 19310
Phone: (610) 593-1777; Fax: (610) 593-2002
E-mail: Info@schifferbooks.com

For the largest selection of fine reference books on this and related subjects, please visit our web site at www.schifferbooks.com. We are always looking for people to write books on new and related subjects. If you have an idea for a book please contact us at the above address.

This book may be purchased from the publisher.
Include $3.95 for shipping.
Please try your bookstore first.
You may write for a free catalog.

In Europe, Schiffer books are distributed by
Bushwood Books
6 Marksbury Ave.
Kew Gardens
Surrey TW9 4JF England
Phone: 44 (0) 20 8392-8585; Fax: 44 (0) 20 8392-9876
E-mail: info@bushwoodbooks.co.uk
Website: www.bushwoodbooks.co.uk
Free postage in the U.K., Europe; air mail at cost.

Contents

Historic Images Through Postcards

Postcards are said to be the most popular collectible history has ever known. The urge to horde them sprang up with the birth of this means of communication at the turn of the twentieth century, and has endured great changes in the printing industry. Today, postcard shows take place every weekend somewhere in the country, or the world, and millions of pieces of ephemera lie in wait for those who collect obscure topics or town views.

Postcards once served as the email of their day. They were the fastest, most popular means of communication beginning in the 1890s in the United States. These timely cards provided a way to send visual scenes through the mail along with brief messages—a way to enchant friends and family with the places travelers visited, to send local scenes, or to share favorite topics of imagery. They even provided the latest breaking news, as images of fires, floods, shipwrecks, and festivals were often available in postcard form within hours of an event. Moreover, mail was delivered to most urban homes in the United States at least twice a day. So someone might send a morning postcard inviting a friend to dinner that evening, and receive an RSVP in time to shop for food.

The messages shared and the beautiful scenes combined to create the timeless appeal of postcards as a collectible. Most importantly, history is recorded by the pictures of the times, moments in time reflecting an alluring past.

Dating Postcards

Pioneer Era (1893-1898): Most pioneer cards in today's collections begin with cards placed on sale at the Columbian Exposition in Chicago on May 1, 1893. These were illustrations on government-printed postal cards and privately-printed souvenir cards. The government cards had the printed one-cent stamp, while souvenir

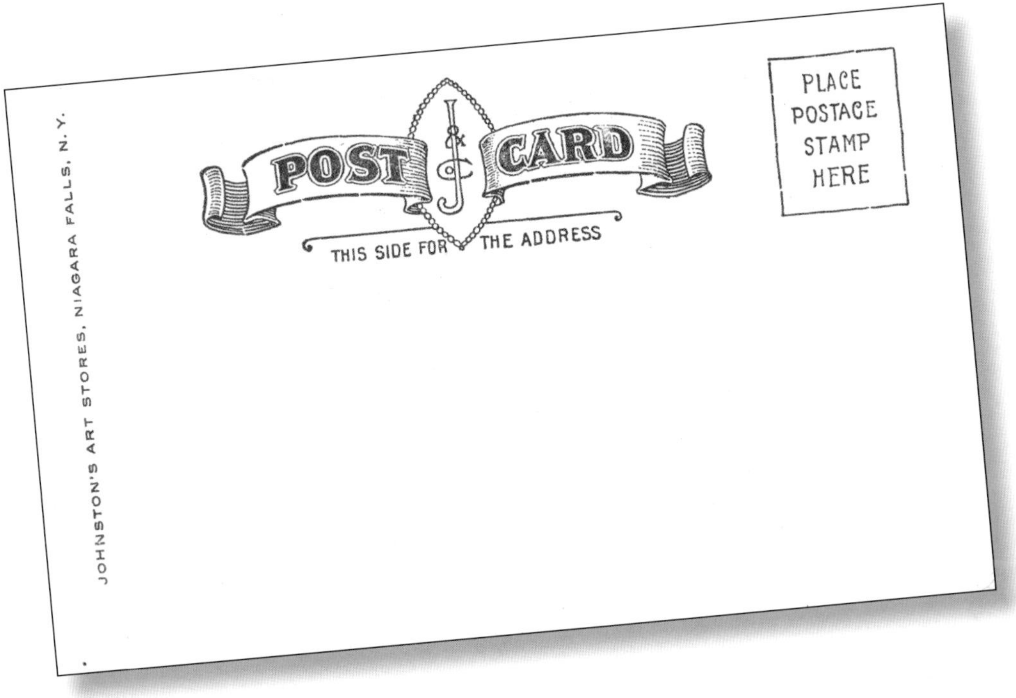

Example of a postcard with an undivided back. Senders could only write the address on this side of the card. Any message needed to be written on the front of the card along with the picture.

cards required a two-cent adhesive postage stamp to be applied. Writing was not permitted on the address side of the card.

Private Mailing Card Era (1898-1901): On May 19, 1898, private printers were granted permission, by an act of Congress, to print and sell cards that bore the inscription, "Private Mailing Card." A one-cent adhesive stamp was required. A dozen or more American printers began to take postcards seriously. Writing was still not permitted on the back.

Post Card Era—Undivided Back (1901-1907): New U. S. postal regulations on December 24, 1901 stipulated that the words "Post Card" should be printed at the top of the address side of privately printed cards. Government-issued cards were to be designated as "Postal Cards." Writing was still not permitted on the address side. In this era, private citizens began to take black and white photographs and have them printed on paper with postcard backs.

Early Divided Back Era (1907-1914): Postcards with a divided back were permitted in Britain in 1902, but not in the United States until March 1, 1907. The address was to be written on the right side; the left side was for writing messages. Many millions of cards were published in this era. Up to this point, most postcards were printed in Germany, which was far ahead of the United States in the use of lithographic processes. With the advent of World War I, the supply of postcards for American consumption switched from Germany to England and the United States.

White Border Era (1915-1930): Most U. S. postcards were printed during this period. To save ink, publishers left a clear border around the view, thus these postcards are referred to as "White Border" cards. The relatively high cost of labor, along with inexperience and changes in public taste, resulted in the production of poor quality cards during this period. Furthermore, strong competition in a narrowing market caused many publishers to go out of business.

Linen Era (1930-1944): New printing processes allowed printing on postcards with high rag content that created a textured finish. These cheap cards allowed the use of gaudy dyes for coloring.

Photochrome Era (1945 to date): "Chrome" postcards began to dominate the scene soon after the Union Oil Company placed them in its western service stations in 1939. Mike Roberts pioneered with his "WESCO" cards soon after World War II. Three-dimensional postcards also appeared in this era.

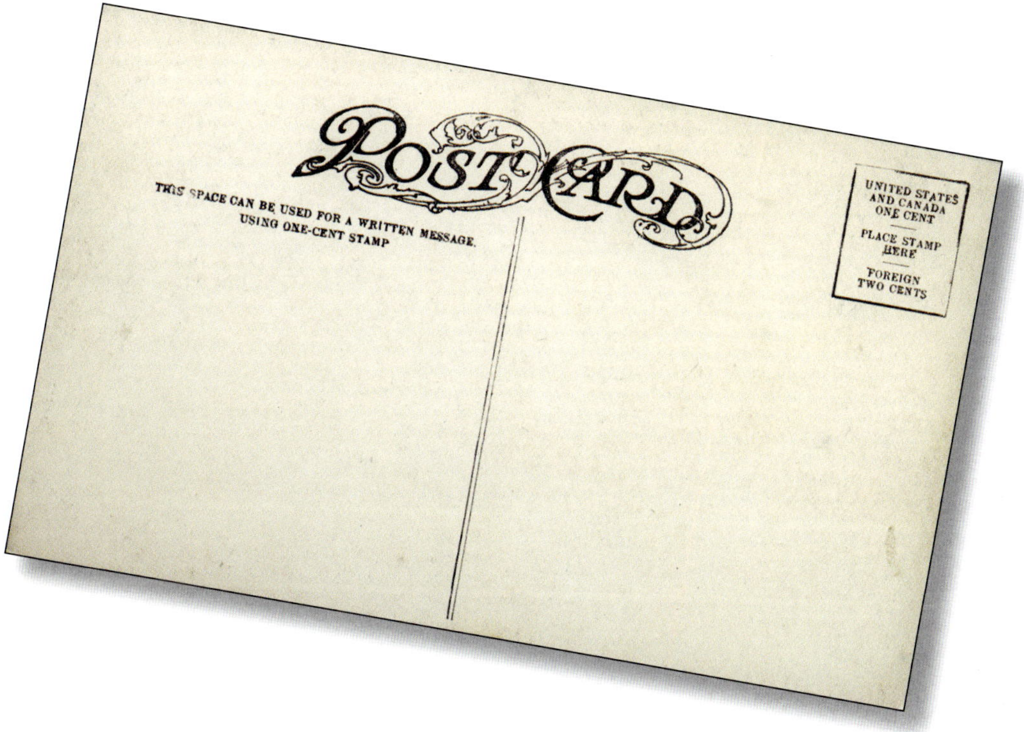

Sample of a postcard with a divided back. Senders were allowed to put an address on the right hand side of the postcard and a message on the left side.

Introduction

It's no secret to those both living in Texas and visiting there, that everyone swells with a state pride that is as important today as it was in yesteryear's culture. Dallas is no different—in fact, the Dallas Convention and Visitors Bureau proudly shares it's timeless slogan: "Live Large. Think Big." In Dallas, all things were—and are—possible.

Being the third largest city in the State and the ninth in the U. S., it's no surprise that the culture and economics of Dallas has always been essential to the nation. It quickly became a major player in the petroleum and cotton industries; and though there is no negotiable connection to the sea, the rails and stage coaches were able to sustain their vast interactions with the rest of the traveling world.

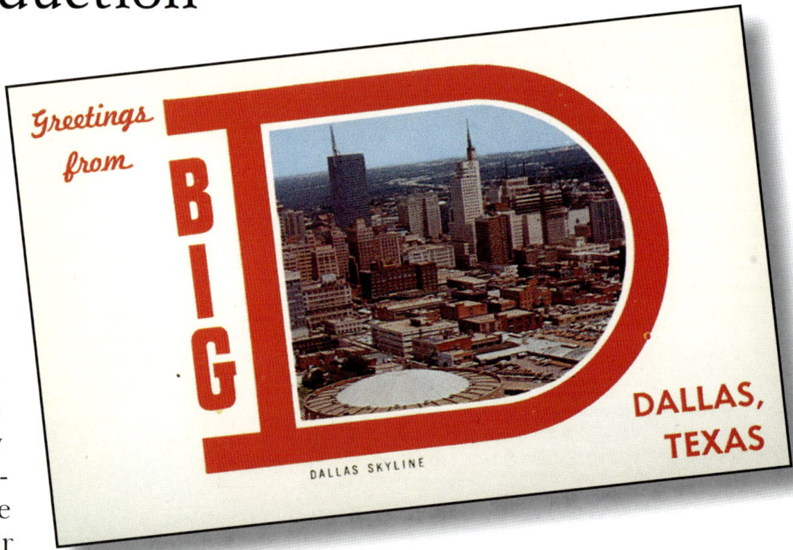

One of the "Big D" letter postcards showing the busy Dallas metropolis. At the turn of the century, postcards and other greetings often displayed black and white images that spelled out varied words and names. Cities, towns, and states followed suit as people found the idea an engaging way to announce where they were visiting to the "folks back home." Most of these cards had the words "Greetings From" preceding the lettered card.

Circa 1950s, $2-4

In the Beginning...

John Neely Bryan came to the area in 1839, with the idea of placing a trading post to serve both the settlers and the Indians living there. The site was a desirable one. Crossing the Trinity River was an enticement and there was also favorable access to the Preston Trail (a passage that would eventually connect north and south Texas). Once Bryan had studied the land, he made the decision to return to his home in Arkansas to resolve his affairs before returning to open the trading post.

But when he returned, in 1841, half his customer base was gone! It was then that he decided to change his initial plan, and to, instead, plan a community. Inviting people from nearby areas, his town began to take on life, and soon, more and more people wanted to settle in Dallas.

What's in a Name?

There is a bit of discrepancy about where the name *Dallas* came from and why it was attached to this thriving community. John Neely Bryan has been quoted as saying that the town was named "after my friend Dallas." But others say different. One candidate for the name is George Mifflin Dallas, the United States' eleventh vice president—though the town was called Dallas many years prior to this election. Varied people think that others are to be attributed with the honor: Commodore Alexander James Dallas (brother of George mentioned prior and stationed in the Gulf of Mexico), Walter R. Dallas (he fought at San Jacinto in Houston), James L. Dallas (Walter's brother, a Texas Ranger), and Joseph Dallas (living in the area a few years after Bryan arrived). A mystery.

Not an Easy Life...

Incorporated as a town in 1856, Dallas grew progressively, with people from other colonies arriving and becoming actively involved in all facets of growth. By 1860, two thousand people called Dallas home.

But prosperous population was not the only thing brought to Dallas in 1860. Political debates about secession spurred the development of a volunteer company in preparation for war. Fire also threw the community into havoc when it broke out, destroying most of the business district. Blame for the blaze was thrown toward slavery abolitionists thus linking the town to war even more closely. Though the city was mostly rebuilt by the end of the year, the growing population saw the beginning of housing shortages.

In 1861, Dallas entered the war effort with significant support from the local citizens. Because the town was so far from the center of the fighting, the townspeople became involved by giving supplies, money, and foodstuff for the war effort. Even a weapons factory was built—and eventually was used to store cotton when the Union Army made their approach to Mississippi and Louisiana.

Reconstruction

Times continued to be tough, and Reconstruction brought on new and harrowing problems never before considered. When Texas slaves were given freedom in 1865, many came to Dallas due to its prosperity—which was still better than many other southern places. The white population became fearful, and so the negatively focused Ku Klux Klan, in 1868, first materialized.

Still, despite the hard-hitting times, Dallas folks rebuilt their fortunes after the war and continued to grow during these Reconstruction years. With the arrival of passenger trains, the population more than doubled (from 3,000 people to 7,000) in 1872, allowing economic growth of great proportions. Dallas could now transport grain, cotton, and other supplies. People could travel from place to place. Tourism fed the development of the city.

Of course, growth presents added concerns in any economic situation. Fair pricing became an issue for the crops grown in Dallas, as shipping costs were oftentimes prohibitive, and crop prices—for cotton specifically—were known to drop significantly. A grand solution, The Farmer's Alliance, in 1877, allowed farms to use a warehouse in Dallas to ship cotton to St. Louis, since freight charges were cheaper. Unfortunately, not backed by the banking community, the undertaking failed in just under two years.

And one cannot forget the outlaw element in this western territory in early years—Doc Holiday, Belle Starr, and Sam Bass (among others).

The Early 1900s

The year 1910 brought an interest in educational development adding to the growing economic trends. The Methodists noticed Dallas and established, by 1915, the Southern Methodist University after the city presented $300,000 and 666.5 acres for the campus.

The Federal Reserve Bank came to Dallas in 1911, solidifying the city as a financial center, and later, World War I brought the aviation industry.

But as with all of Texas, Dallas is known for its oil. Discovered 100 miles east of Dallas in 1930, by Columbus

Marion Joiner, the oil industry eased the suffering of the Great Depression for those living in the city. This further empowered the business and financial communities—and Dallas never looked back!

A Grieving City…

Of course, 1963 was a pivotal moment in time for Dallas. On November 22nd, near the spot where John Neely Bryan had first called home, President John F. Kennedy was assassinated by Lee Harvey Oswald, spurring controversy that still plagues America today. Oswald was killed two days later by a Dallas nightclub owner, Jack Ruby.

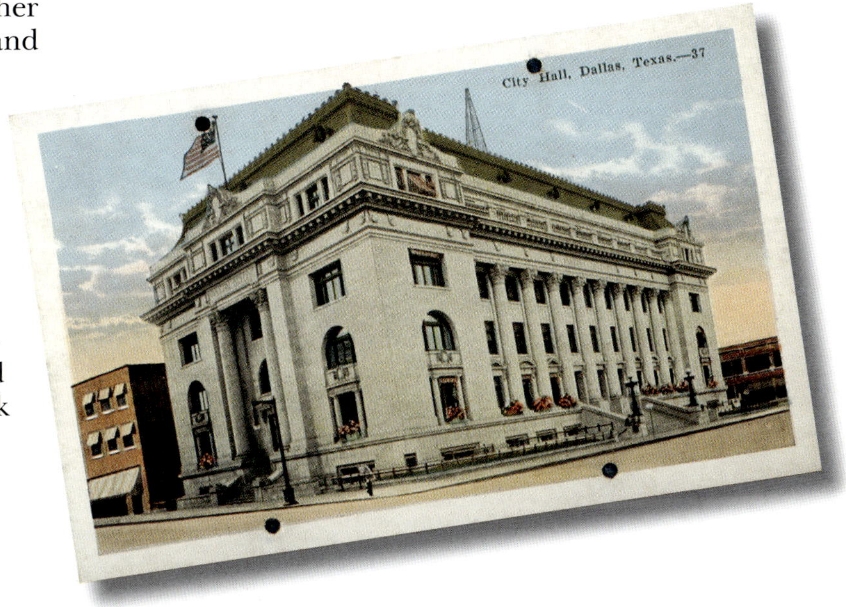

Located on South Harwood Street from 1912 to 1978, the old Dallas City Hall was the setting for the 1963 assassination of Lee Harvey Oswald.

Circa 1914, $2-4

Public Postcards

The economics of Dallas has not been slighted when it comes to growth of public and civic responsibility. Government buildings and schools have been built, rebuilt, and upgraded through the years. The State Fair has developed and become an extravaganza of wondrous proportions. The population has flourished giving Dallas the reputation of a diverse and thriving town.

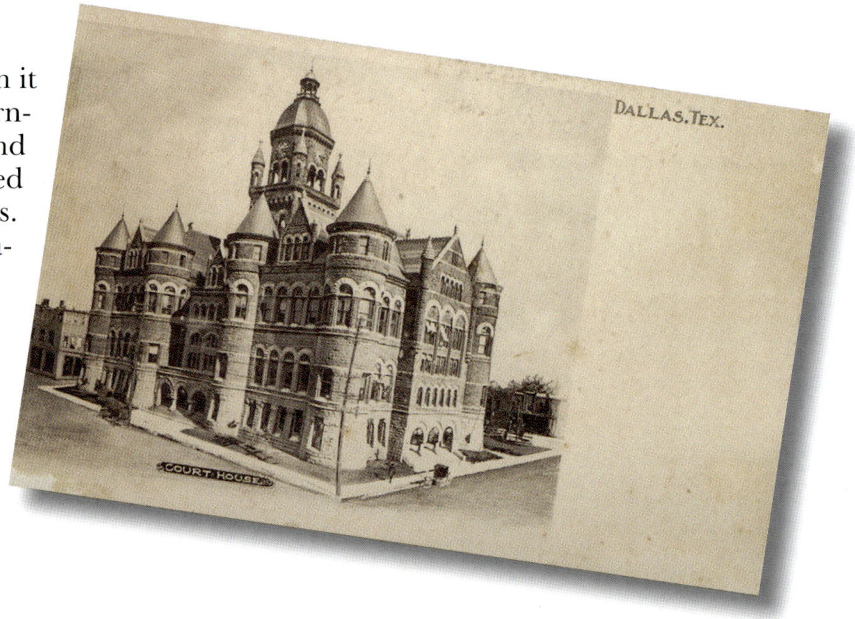

Called the Old Red Courthouse, this postcard view shows the red sandstone and blue granite building on Houston Street. Fifth in line to dwell in this location, it was designed by Orlopp and Kusener, costing $300,000.

Circa early 1900s, $6-8

Government and Public Buildings

From the Dallas City Hall to the Confederate Monument, government and public buildings grace the pages of a historic time, rich with the color of pride.

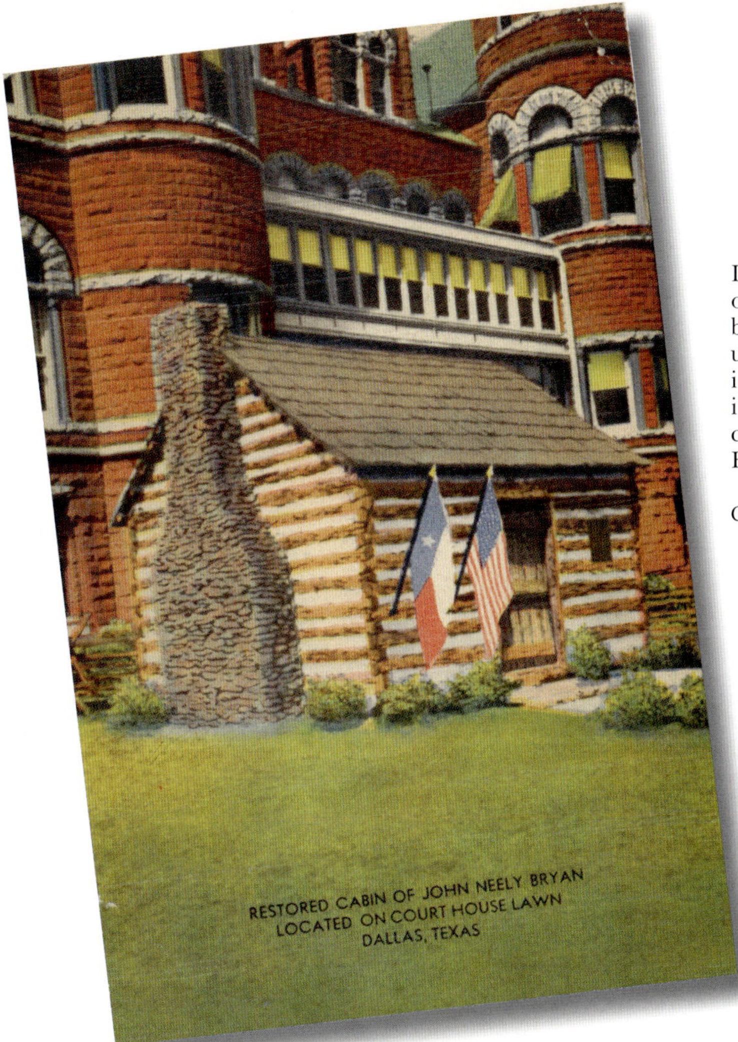

In 1846, John Neely Bryan organized Dallas County, bringing the first post office under the Republic of Texas in 1843-1846, and (shown in the background of the cabin) the first County Court House's cabin, built in 1841.

Circa 1930s, $2-4

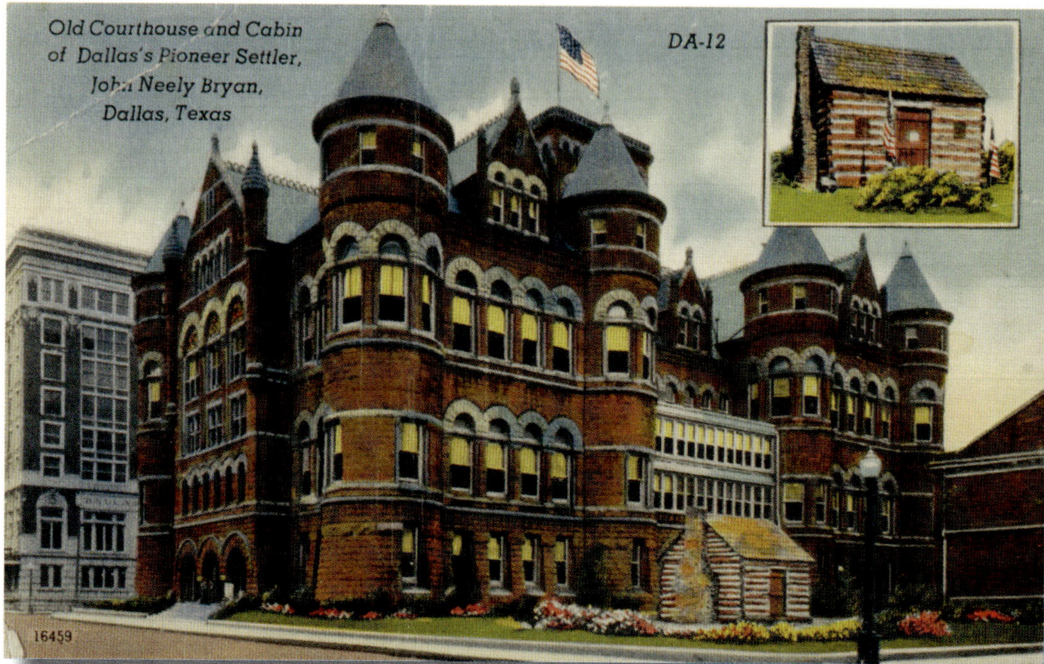

In 1919, a clock tower was removed from the court house building because it was feared that vibrations from the bell might damage the structure. Inset in this postcard is the Cabin of John Neely Bryan, located on the front lawn. Bryan, a pioneer and businessman, was not only founder of Dallas, but donated the courthouse property to the city.

Circa 1930s, $2-4

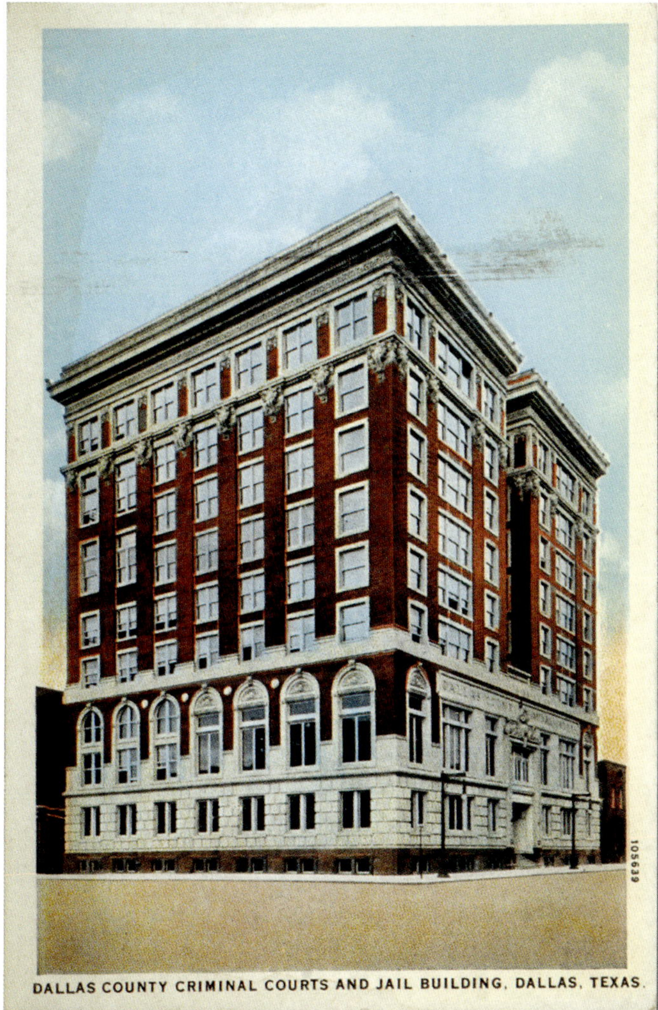

DALLAS COUNTY CRIMINAL COURTS AND JAIL BUILDING, DALLAS, TEXAS.

The Dallas County Criminal Courts and Jail Building, located at Houston and Main Streets, was built in 1913. It was thought to be escape proof due to its eight-story construction. The infamous Jack Ruby trial was held in one of the courtrooms in this building.

Circa 1914, $4-6

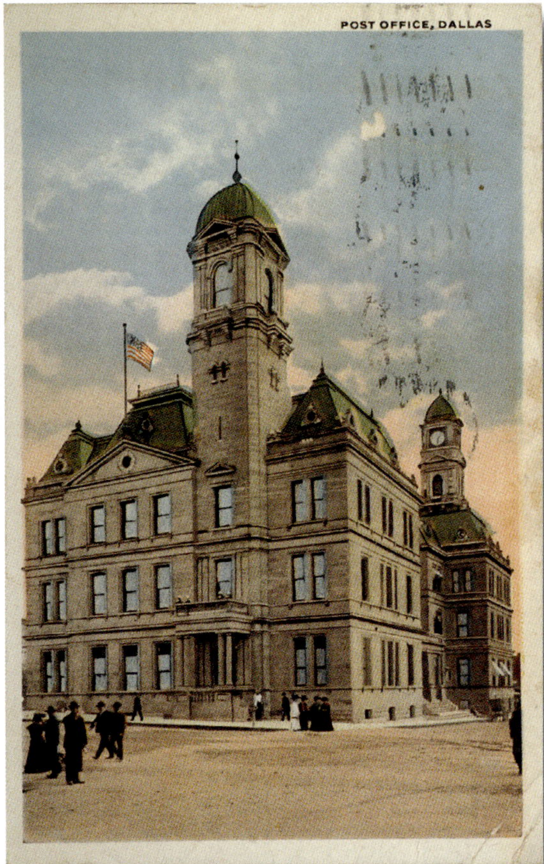

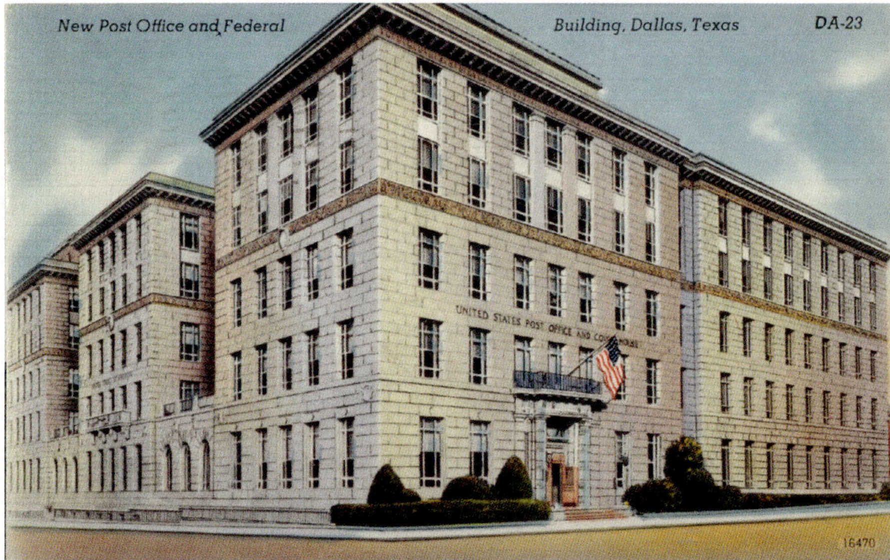

The number of residents for Dallas in 1900 was about 42,000 in number, but the Dallas Post Office was handling mail for a city with twice that number. This view is of a newer postal center, federal building, and courthouse.

Cancelled 1944, $4-6

Dallas, in the late 1800s, had an active mail delivery schedule, mainly because they'd left the stage lines behind for the railroad's ease of use.

Cancelled 1918, $4-6

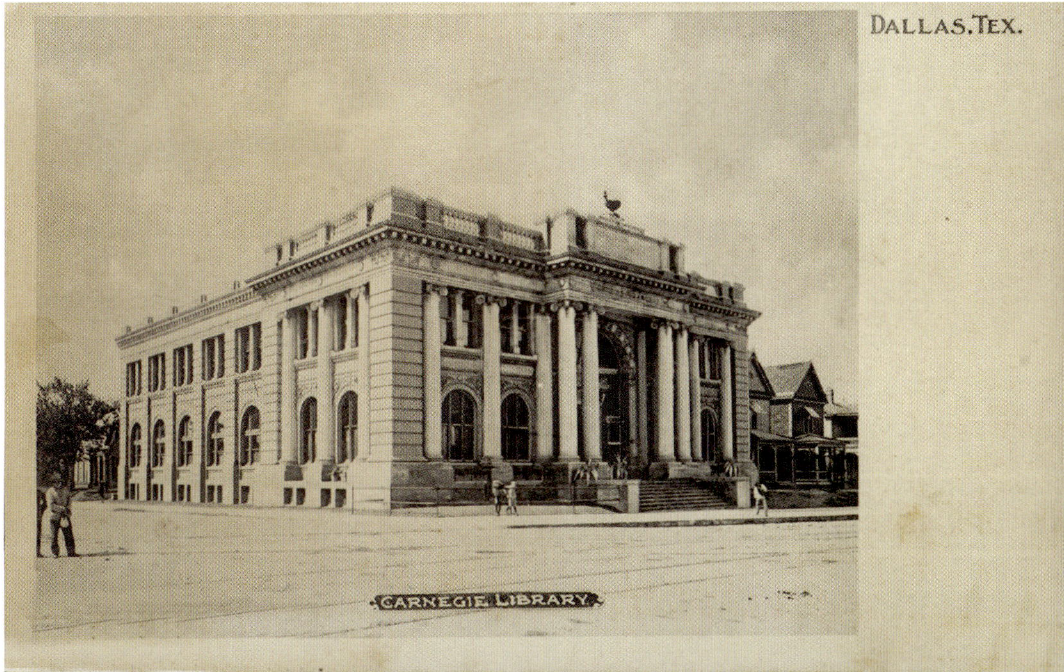

May Dickson, a civic volunteer for the Dallas Federation of Women's Clubs, helped to raise $11,000 in 1899 to build a public library. This came to fruition when Andrew Carnegie gave one if his famous library grants to Dallas in the amount of $50,000.

Circa early 1900s, $6-8

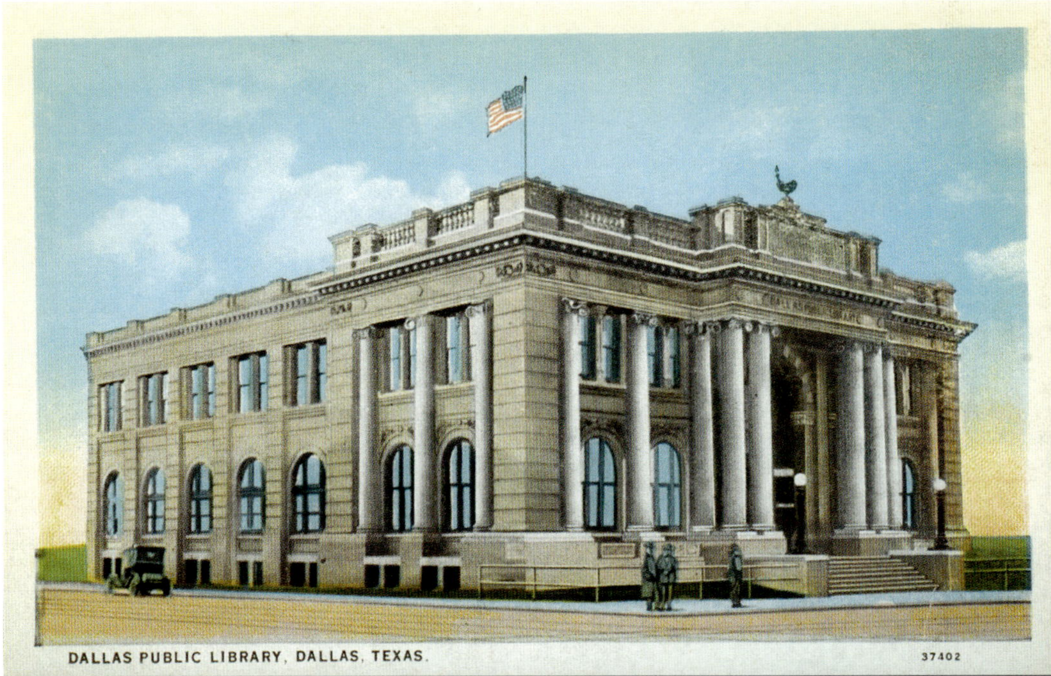

The library opened at the corner of Commerce and Harwood Streets in October of 1901. This building included an Art Room on the second floor. The Dallas Museum of Art later exhibited the artwork from this gallery as a premier focal point.

Circa 1914, $4-6

The State Fair

The Dallas State Fair and Exposition was first chartered in 1886 by a group of Dallas businessmen (W. H. Gaston, John S. Armstrong, Thomas L. Marsalis, James B. Simpson, Sidney Smith, to name a few) to set up industry displays.

There were problems at first, as with most big projects. W. H. Gaston proposed having the fair within the modern borders of Fair Park. But resistance arose from those wanting a location that favored farming entities. Eventually, when no agreement was forthcoming, the opposers chartered a separate event to be held north of the town—one day ahead of the Dallas State Fair.

Oddly enough, both fairs attracted crowds with attendance estimating to be over 100,000 people. Unfortunately, the success did not translate to dollars and cents, and both fairs failed to meet their expenses. Finally, the two groups merged in 1887, and became the Texas State Fair and Dallas Exposition. The fairgrounds were expanded.

In 1904, the city of Dallas purchased the grounds to use as a public park, and in 1936, hosted the Texas Centennial Exposition. The buildings that are presently seen on the grounds were built for this specialized event. The next year also proved successful when Dallas held the Greater Texas and Pan-American Exposition. Dallas fairs had become a staple for the city!

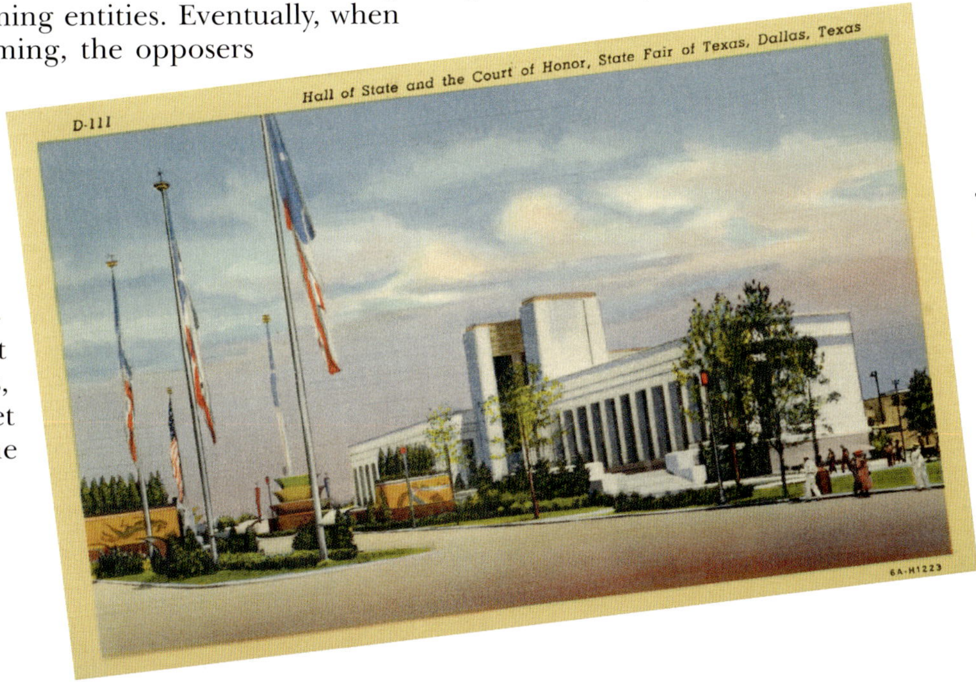

The State of Texas Building was built in 1936 as a monument to the people of the entire State of Texas. Donald Barthleme was the famed architect of this magnificent building.

Circa 1930s, $2-4

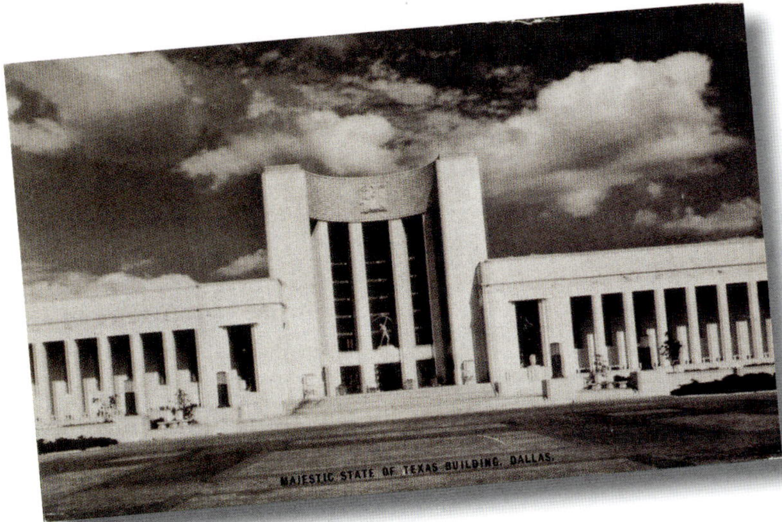

One of the most costly buildings (per square foot) of any Texas building, this majestic structure's price tag was $1,200,000.

Circa early 1900s, $6-8

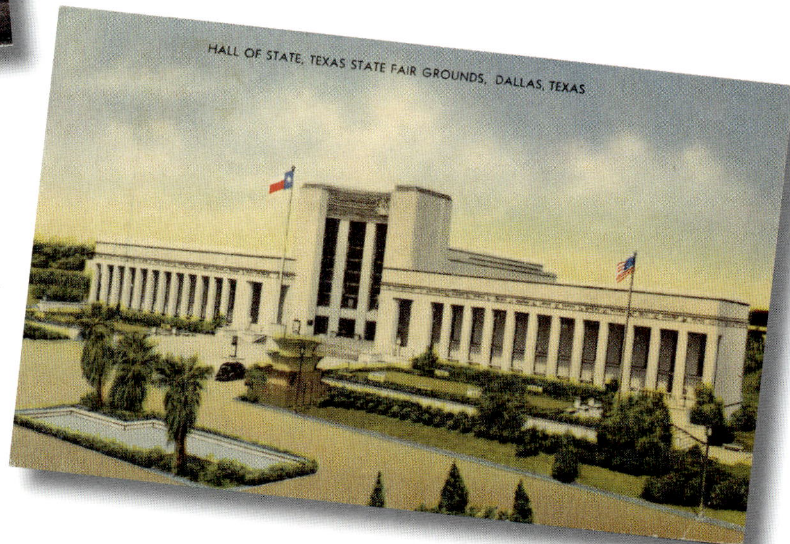

Built of limestone, it includes designs from many artists—all in the name of the Texans who built an empire out of a great wilderness.

Cancelled 1945, $2-4

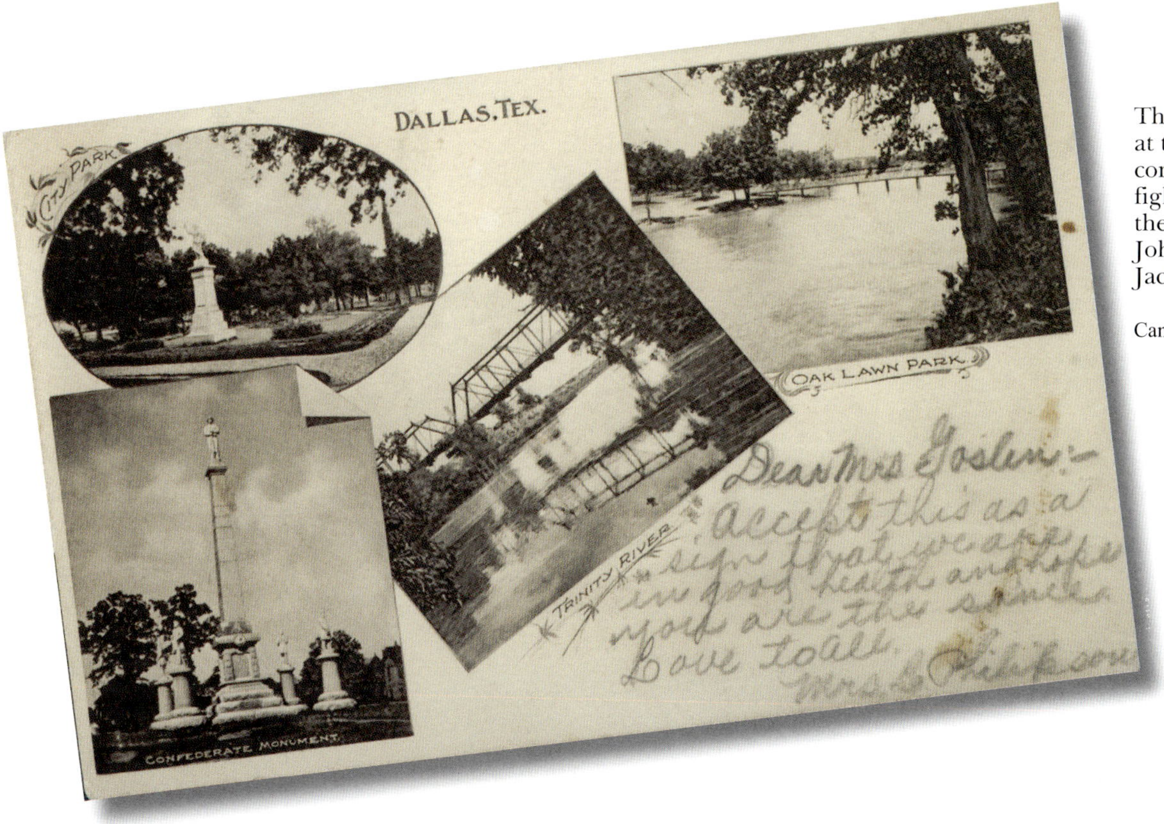

The Confederate Monument shown at the bottom left of this view commemorates four great leaders fighting as Confederates during the American Civil War—Albert Johnston, Robert E. Lee, Stonewall Jackson, and Jefferson Davis.

Cancelled 1905, $6-8

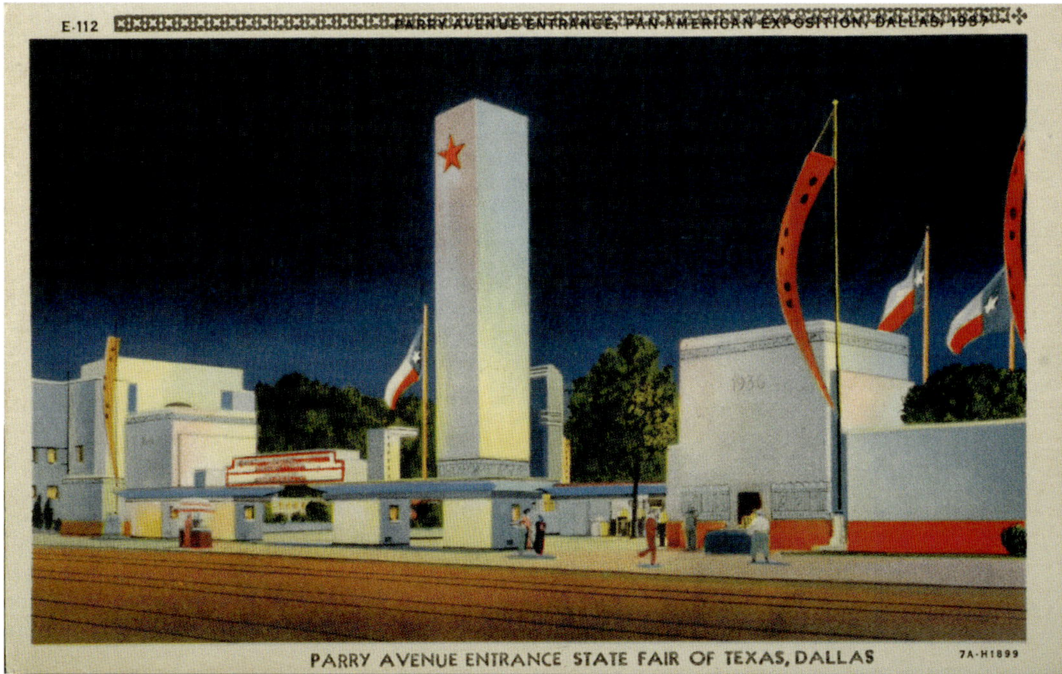

Circa 1914, $4-6

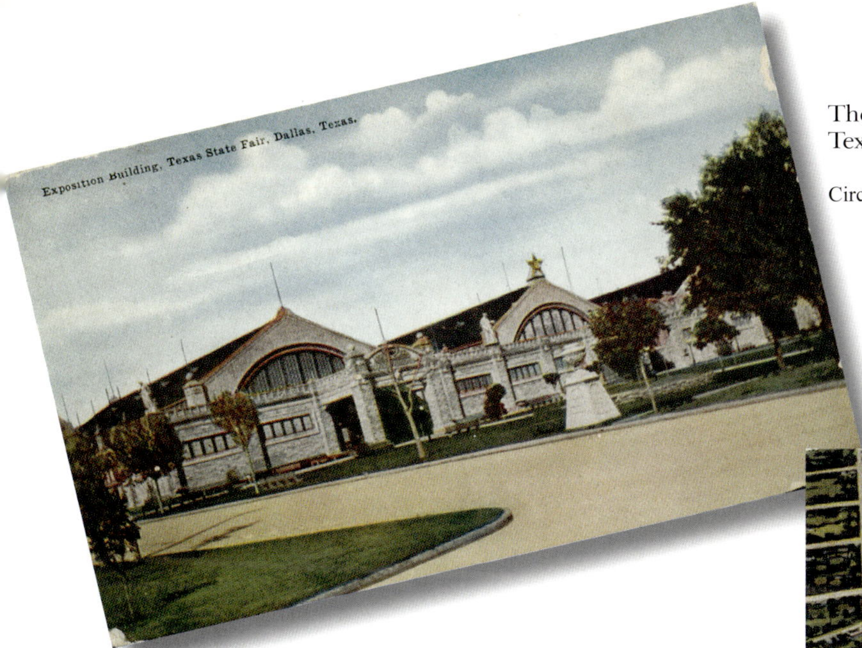

The Exposition Building at the Texas State Fair.

Circa 1910, $2-4

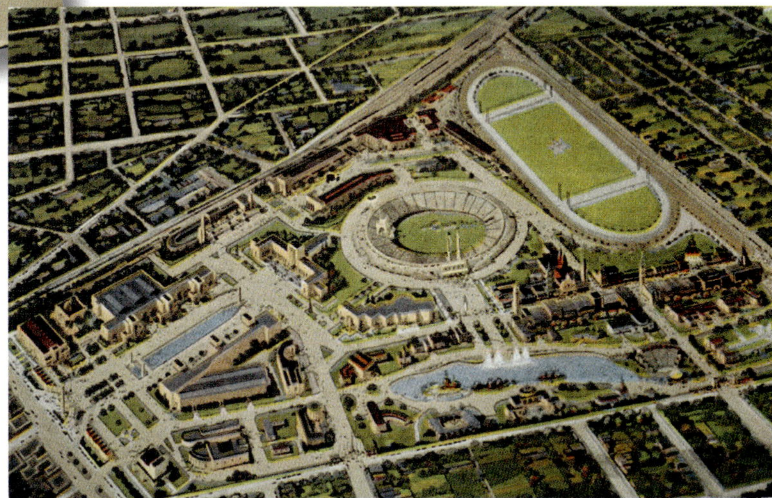

A bird's-eye-view of the Texas Centennial Exposition celebrating Texas' 100th birthday and "commemorating its glamorous past and its achievements subsequent to the birth of the Republic of Texas in 1836."

Circa early 1900s, $2-4

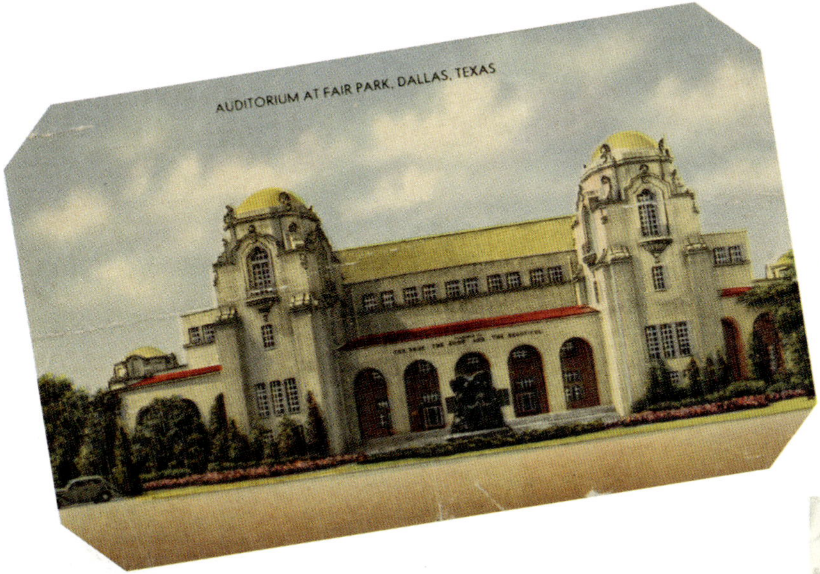

The Auditorium at Fair Park had a seating capacity of 4,300 people and was a main source of entertainment productions at the Texas State Fair. The Metropolitan Opera Association visited annually.

Cancelled 1947, $2-4

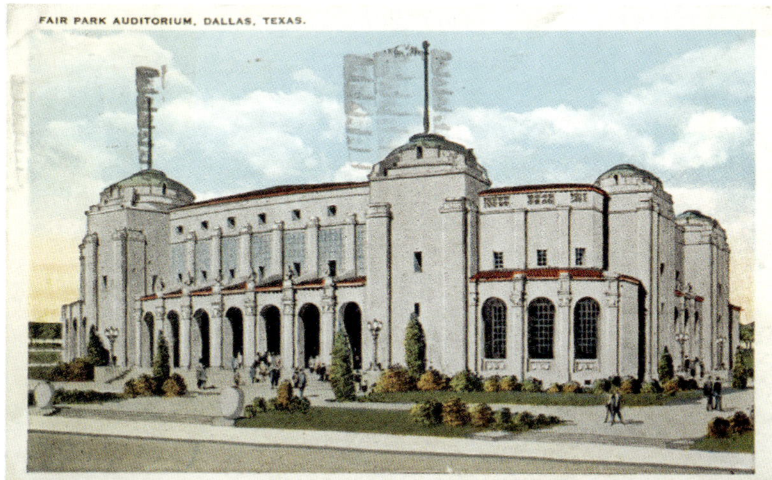

The Auditorium was dedicated to:
The True, The Good, and The Beautiful.

Cancelled 1925, $4-6

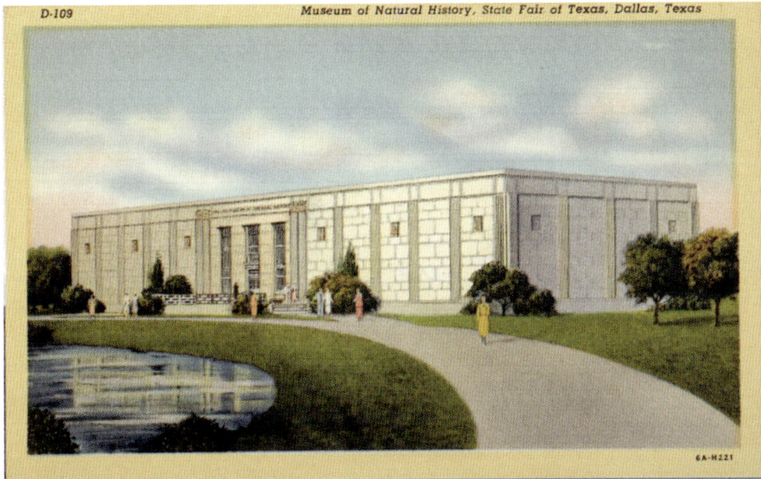

The Museum of Natural History (now called the Museum of Nature and Science) was founded as part of the Texas Centennial in 1936. Not only is this museum now in the National Register of Historic Places, but it has also earned (in 1999) Smithsonian Institution Affiliate Museum status.

Circa 1914, $2-4

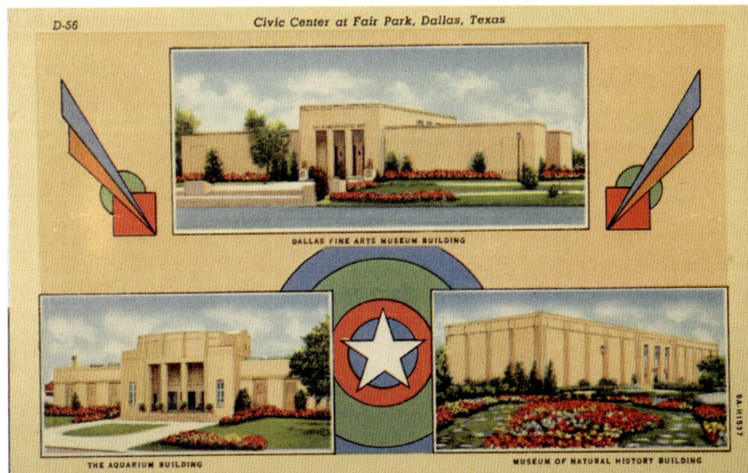

This postcard shows the Civic Center at Fair Park and two of the attraction buildings. The Museum of Natural History exhibits collections from all parts of the state. Costing $200,000 to build, it is made of native Texas stone.

Cancelled 1941, $2-4

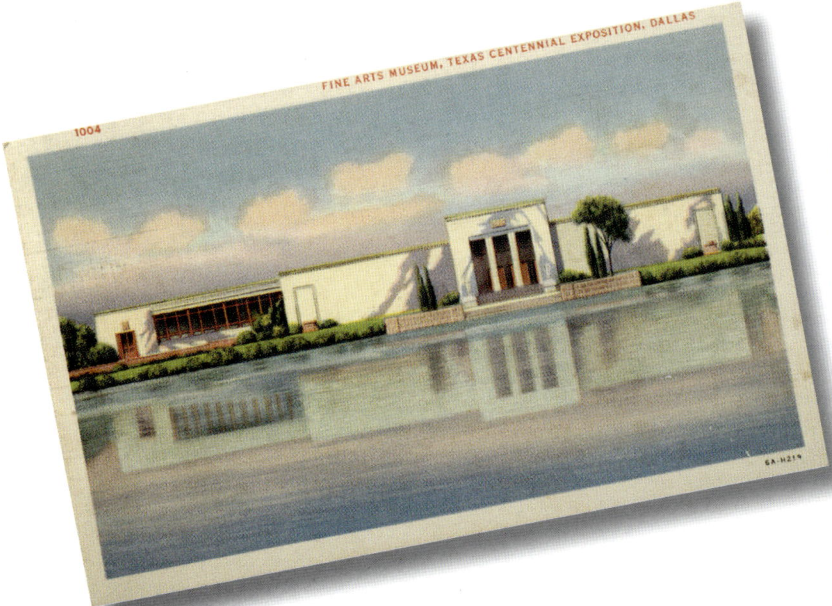

The Fine Arts Museum exhibits art collections from around the world. It has been considered to be one of the most impressive buildings of the Civic Center complex.

Cancelled 1936, $2-4

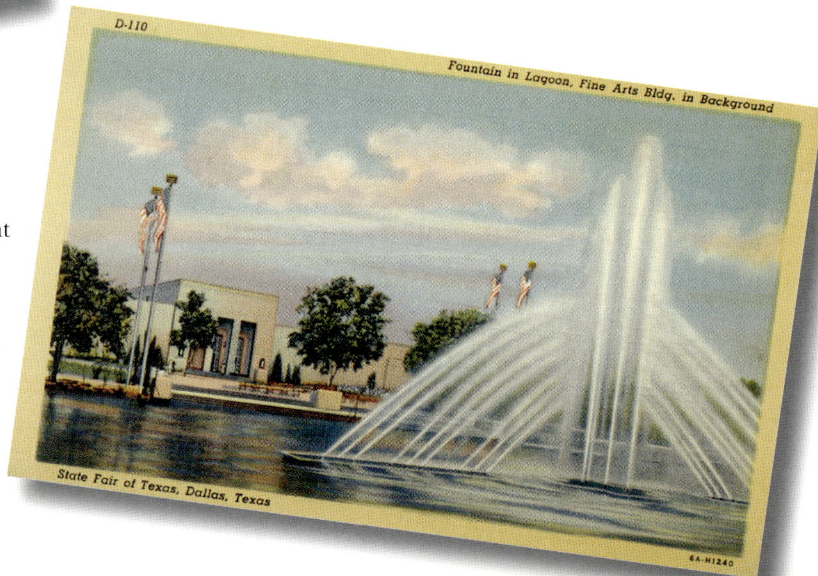

The glorious fountain in front of the Fine Arts Building at the State Fair of Texas.

Circa 1914, $2-4

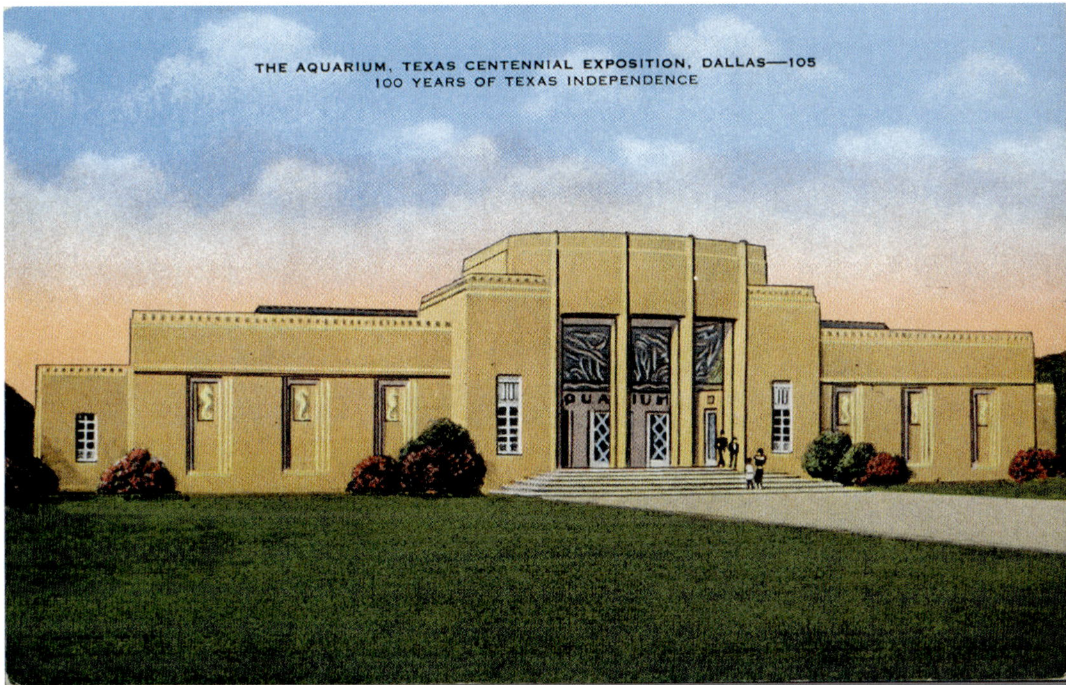

Also part of the Civic Center group, the Aquarium exhibits thousands of species of freshwater fish and was noted as the second aquarium west of the Mississippi, costing $150,000 to build.

Circa 1914, $4-6

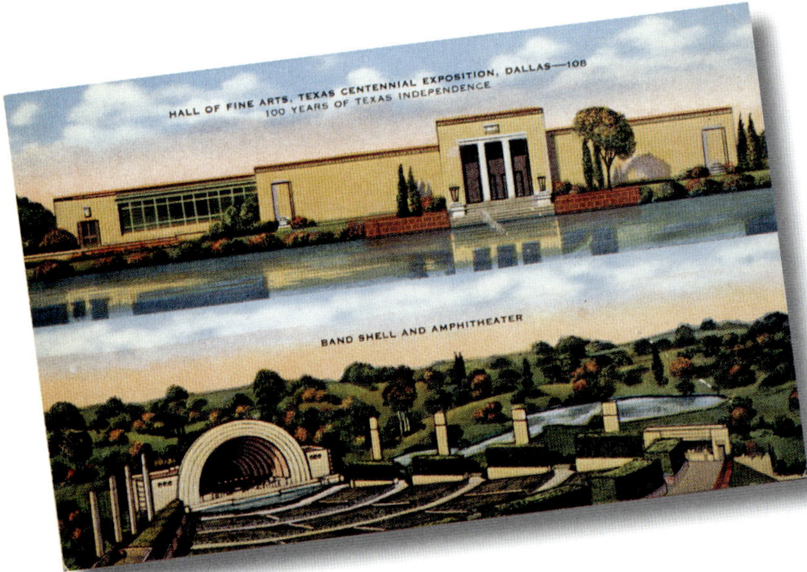

The Band Shell and Amphitheater was an open-air music extravaganza, also a feature of the Civic Center, with the ability to house a 150-piece band and able to seat 5,000 people.

Circa 1914, $2-4

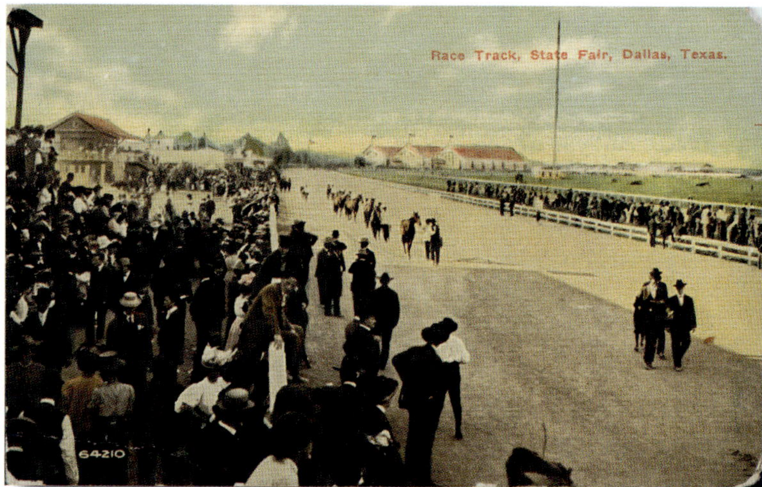

The well-known race track at the State Fair had grandstands that would seat approximately 25,000 people.

Circa 1914, $4-6

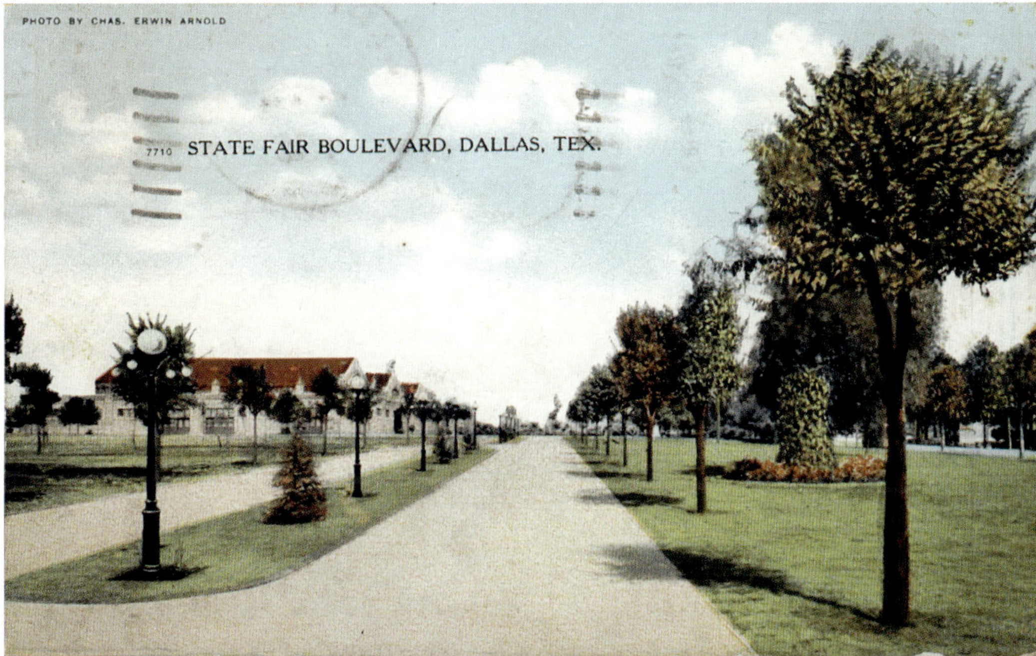

State Fair Boulevard, showing a quiet roadway.

Cancelled 1948, $2-4

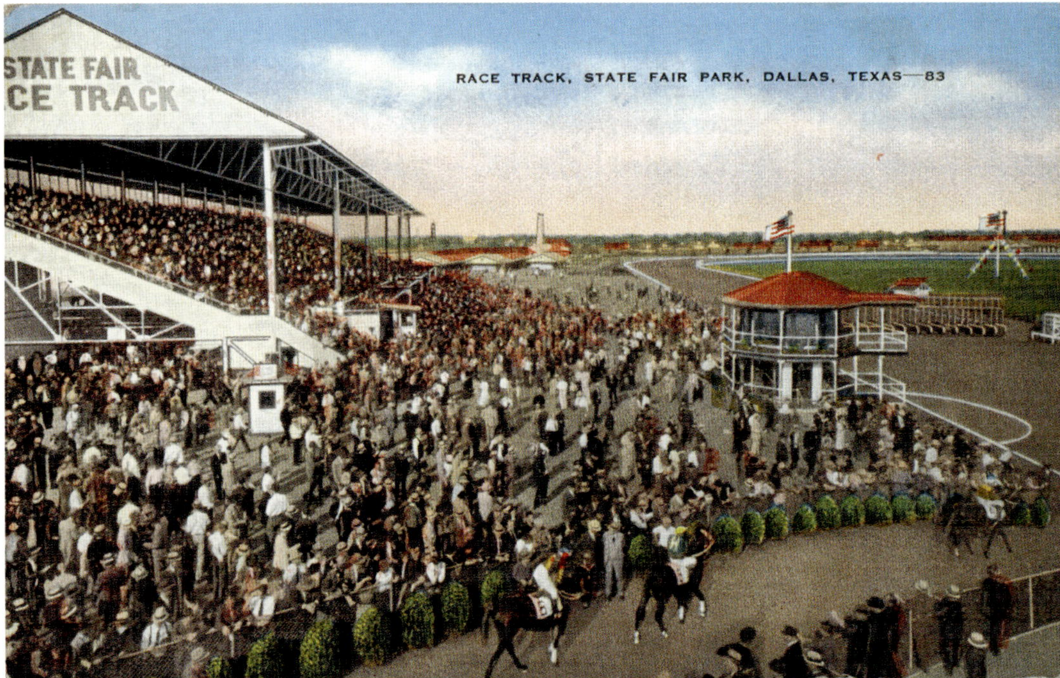

This particular image represents Arlington Downs, developed by W. T. Waggoner's Estate (formed in 1923) with a cost of over $2,000,000. At one time, Waggoner's ranch spread out across more than 500,000 acres in north Texas.

Circa 1914, $2-4

Medical Facilities

With the boom of population always comes the need for healthcare and ways to provide for medical needs. Here, see a varied offering of medical venues that have brought Dallas to its current face for healthcare.

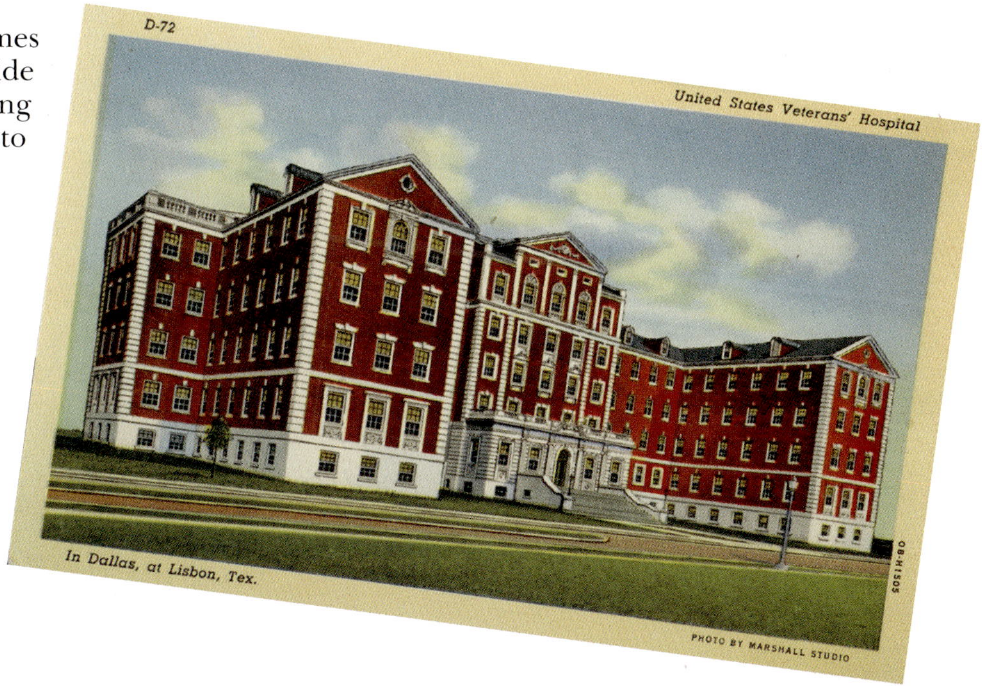

The United States Veterans' Hospital. From the card: *The main building of the immense Hospital Plant, which occupies a 245 acre site, adjoining the city limits at Lisbon.*

Circa 1914, $4-6

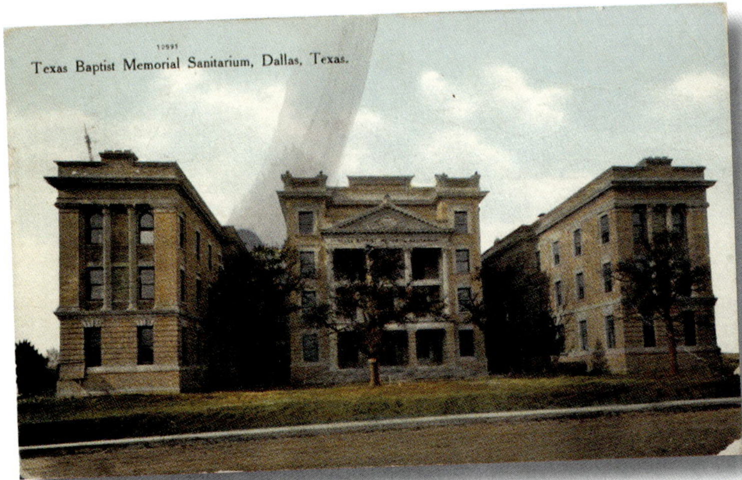

In 1903, the Texas Baptist Memorial Sanitarium was chartered by the Texas Baptist General Convention with a new facility built in 1909. In 1921, it was renamed Baylor Hospital, and since 1959, has been known as the Baylor University Medical Center.

Cancelled 1911, $4-6

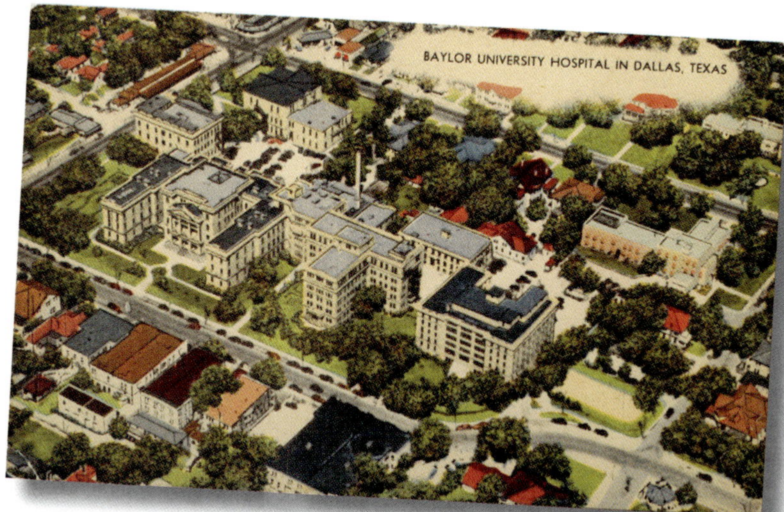

The Baylor University Hospital was originally created as a twenty-five-bed hospital, but grew to be among the first 100 general hospitals in size in the U.S. It was the twelfth largest church hospital in the nation, as well. Baylor Hospital is the birthplace of the famous Blue Cross Plan of Group Hospitalization.

Circa 1914, $2-4

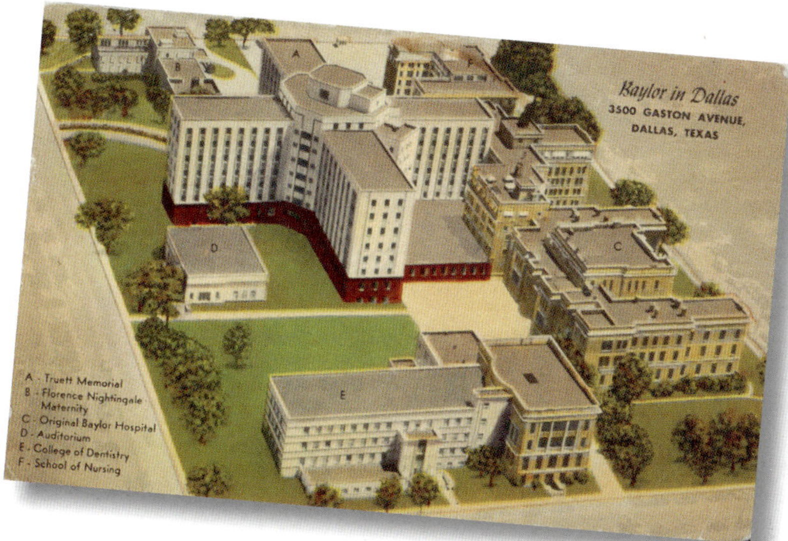

Showing the varied buildings at the Baylor Hospital, it was noted that the George W. Truett Memorial Building (shown as *A* on the card) offered 450 beds, bringing the total capacity, at that time, to 860 beds for those needing hospitalization.

Cancelled 1953, $4-6

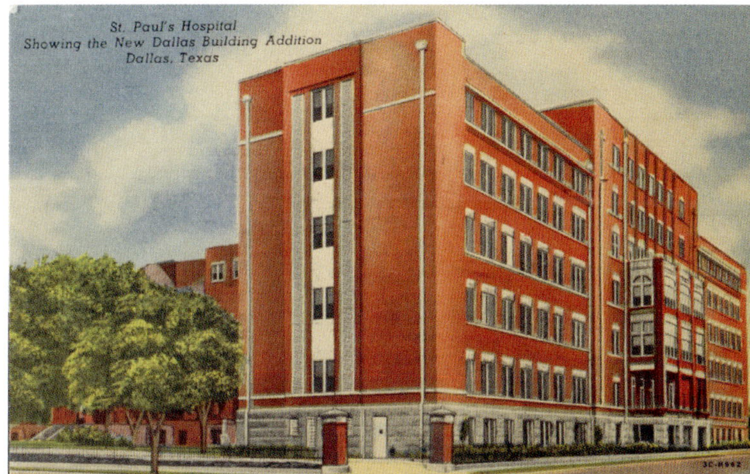

St. Paul's Hospital was owned and operated, in 1936, by the Daughters of Charity of St. Vincent De Paul. The Daughters of Charity is an organization with chapters in Arkansas, Louisiana, Missouri, and Texas providing assistance (and today funding) to create healthy communities for the poor and underserved.

Circa 1930s,$2-4

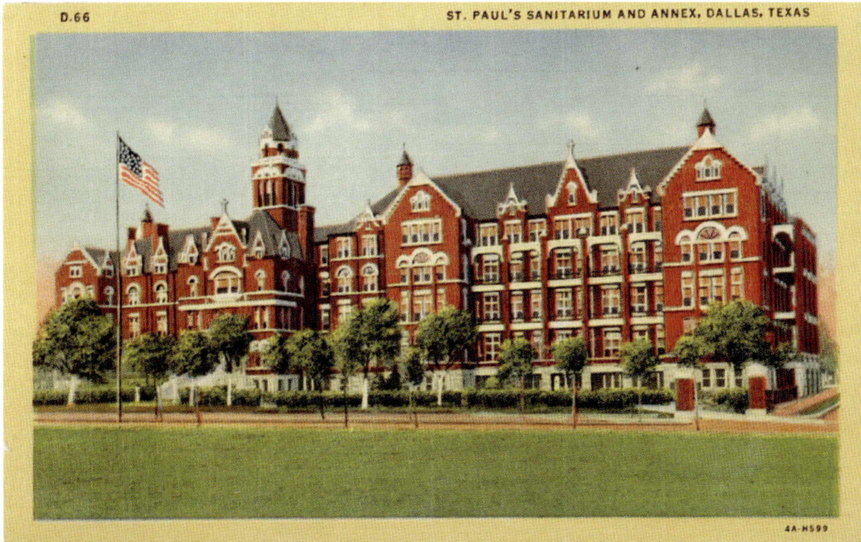

St. Paul's Sanitarium and Annex.

Circa 1914, $2-4

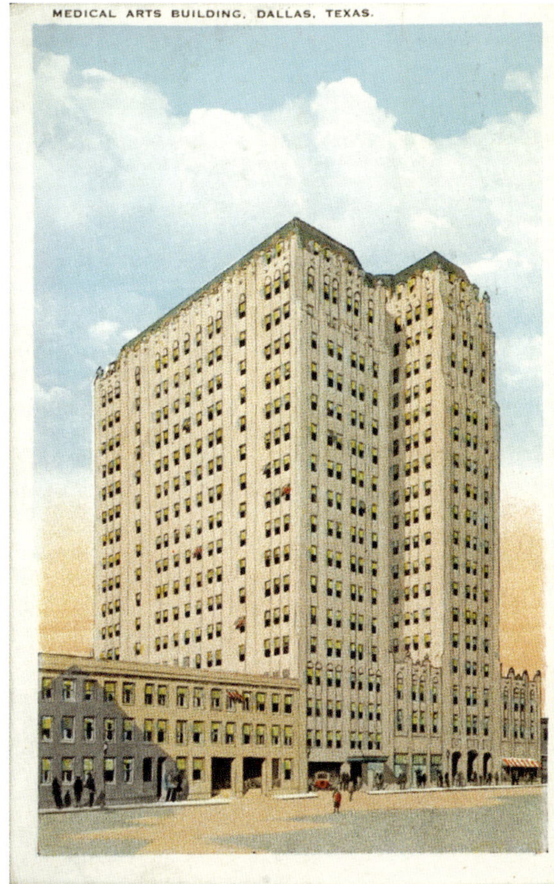

The Medical Arts Building—a high-rise in Dallas.

Cancelled 1931, $2-4

Schools, Religious Colleges, Churches, and Organizations

Educational facilities have always been important to the Dallas culture. Many shown here are religious based, displaying the strong connection between God and man for the population.

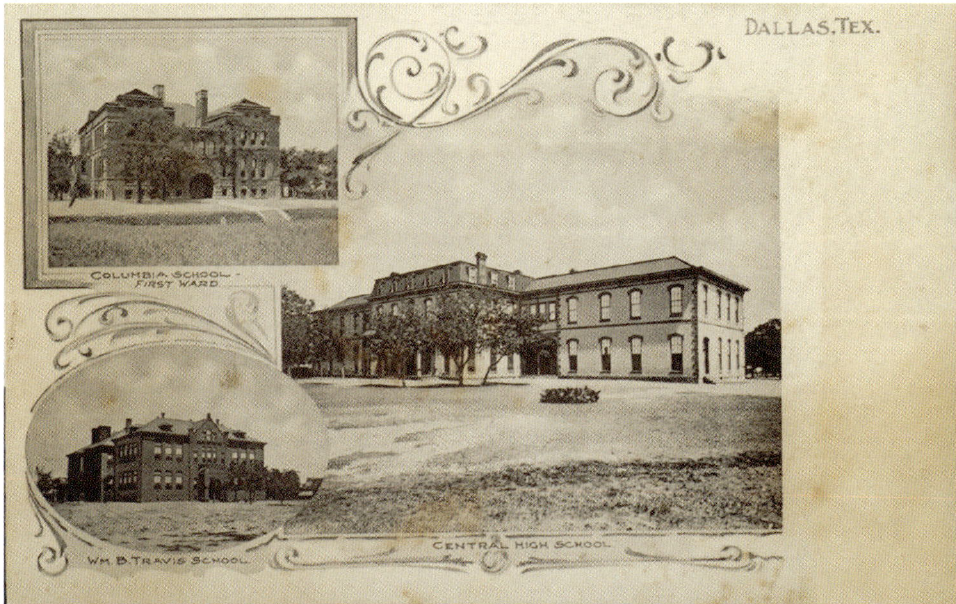

Here, the Central High School, Columbia School, and the William B. Travis School. The namesake, William B. Travis, commanded at the Battle of Alamo during the Texas Revolution and is famous for an uplifting letter of honor and courage, saying "I shall never surrender or retreat."

Circa early 1900s, $6-8

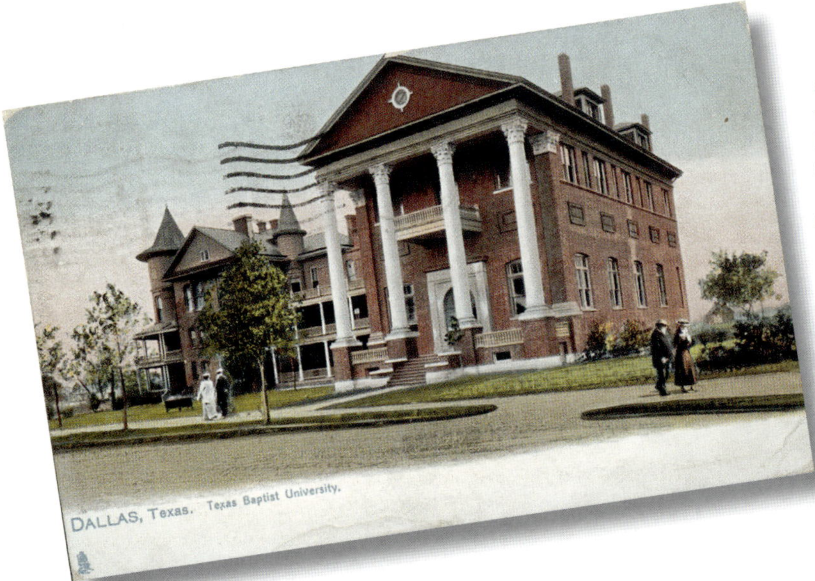

Chartered in 1881, the Texas Baptist University was located on the south bank of the Trinity River making it different from the "professional" schools located within the city.

Cancelled 1907, $8-10

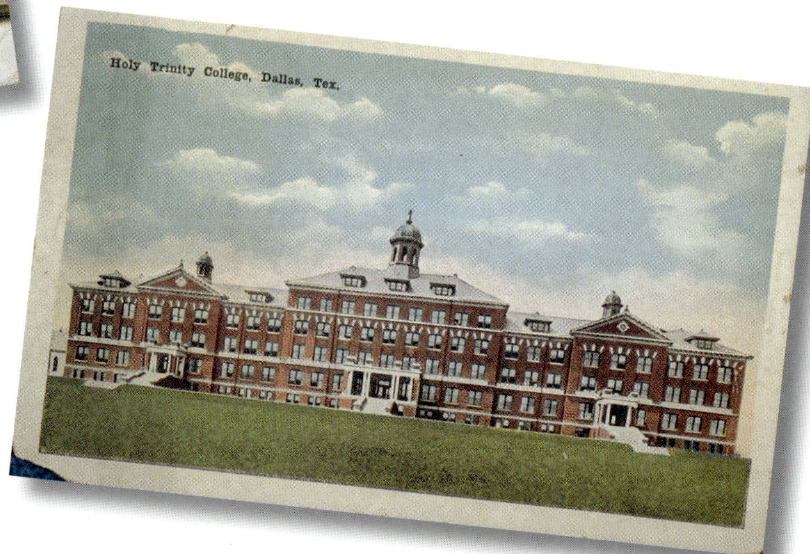

The Holy Trinity College in Dallas became, in the early 1940s, a Jesuit High School—initially serving 195 students.

Circa 1914, $4-6

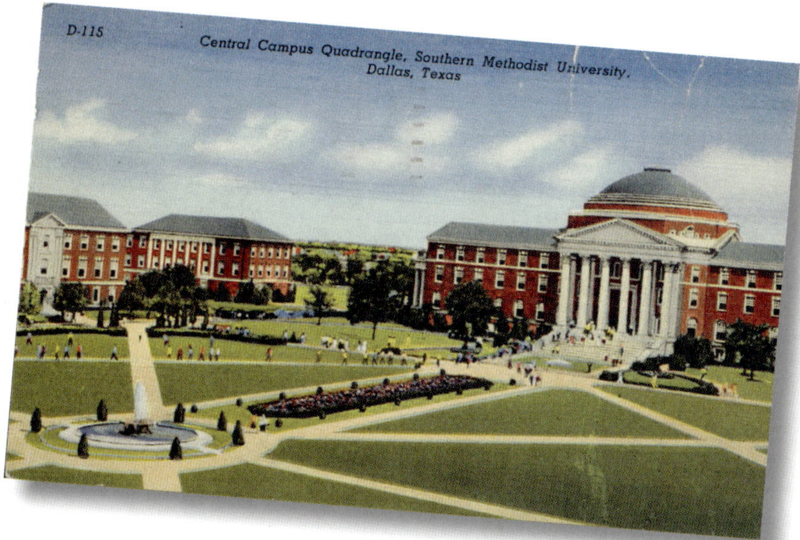

The United Methodist Church founded the Southern Methodist University in 1911 as an educational facility of non-sectarian nature.

Cancelled 1937, $2-4

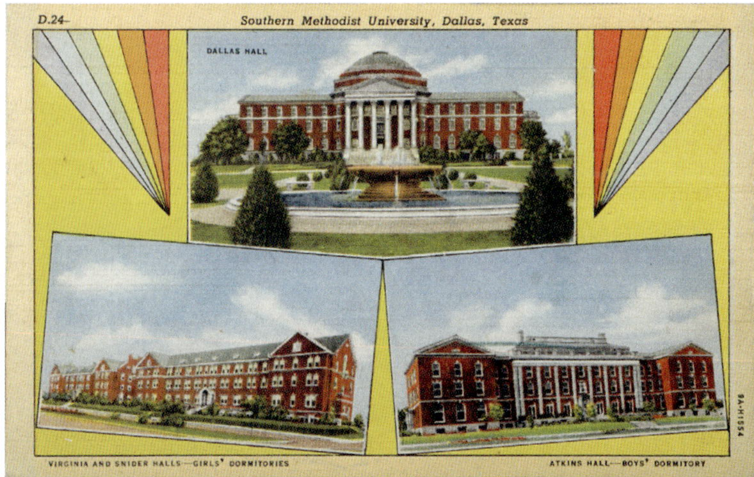

The University opened its doors in 1915 with a motto of being committed to freedom of inquiry.

Circa 1914, $2-4

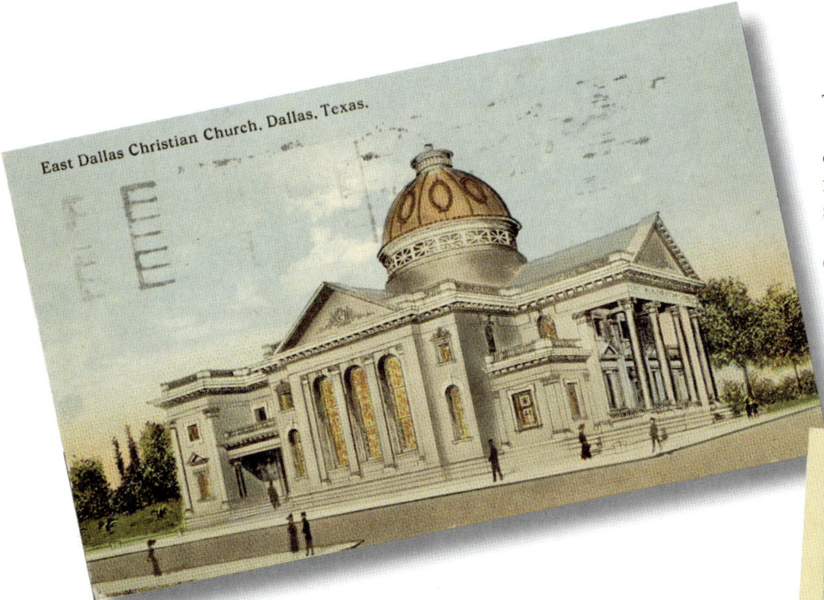

The East Dallas Christian Church was organized in 1903. Beginning as a frame church, it was dedicated on the site located at Victor and Peak Streets. It was moved four years later to Junius and Peak Streets, and stands there today.

Cancelled 1914, $4-6

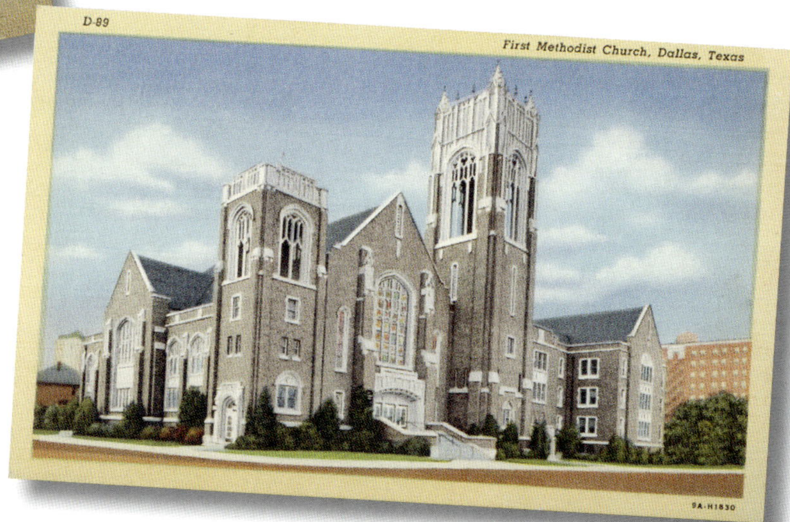

The Trinity Methodist and First Methodist combined congregations in 1916, and created a downtown house of worship in 1921 through member giving. The first service was held in 1926.

Circa 1914, $2-4

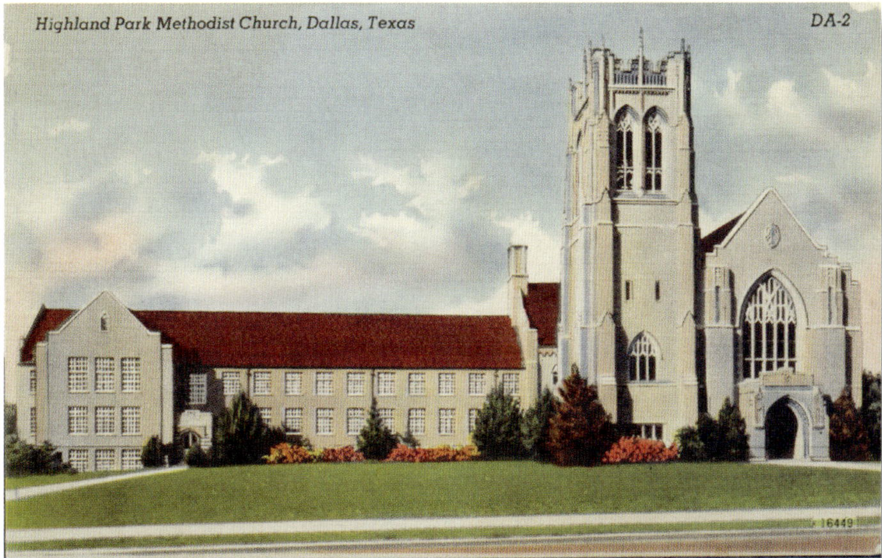

The Highland Park Methodist Church was founded as the University Church (of the Southern Methodist University) in 1916, but changed names soon after when families in Highland Park agreed to transfer their memberships to this congregation. The congregation moved to a first location in 1917—remembered as the Little Brown Church. In 1926, construction of the current church, shown in this postcard, began.

Circa 1930s,$4-6

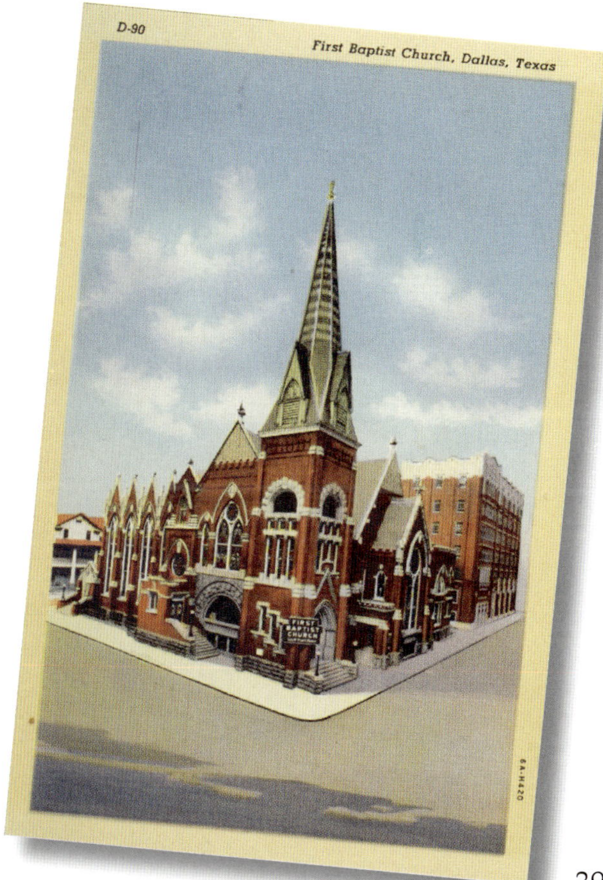

This view of the First Baptist Church shows the second facility, erected in 1891—the congregation outgrew their prior building constructed in 1872.

Circa 1914, $2-4

The Gaston Avenue Baptist Church is now known as the Gaston Oaks Baptist Church.

Cancelled 1913, $4-6

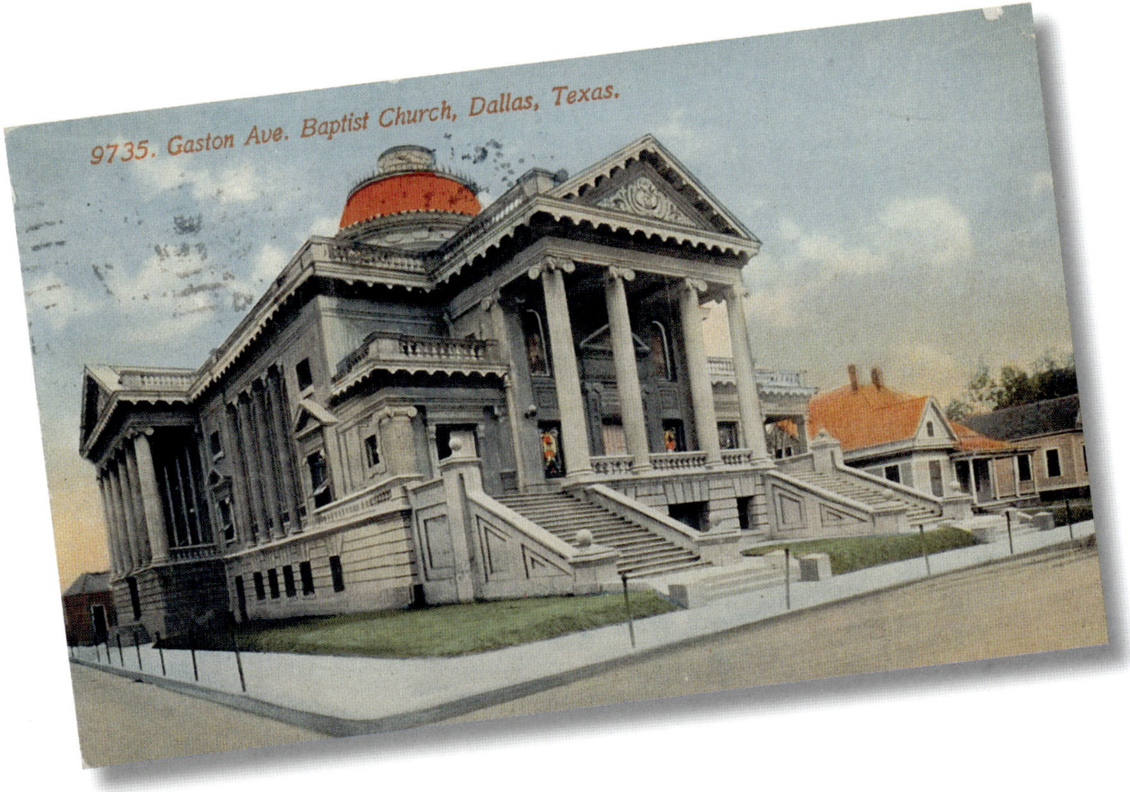

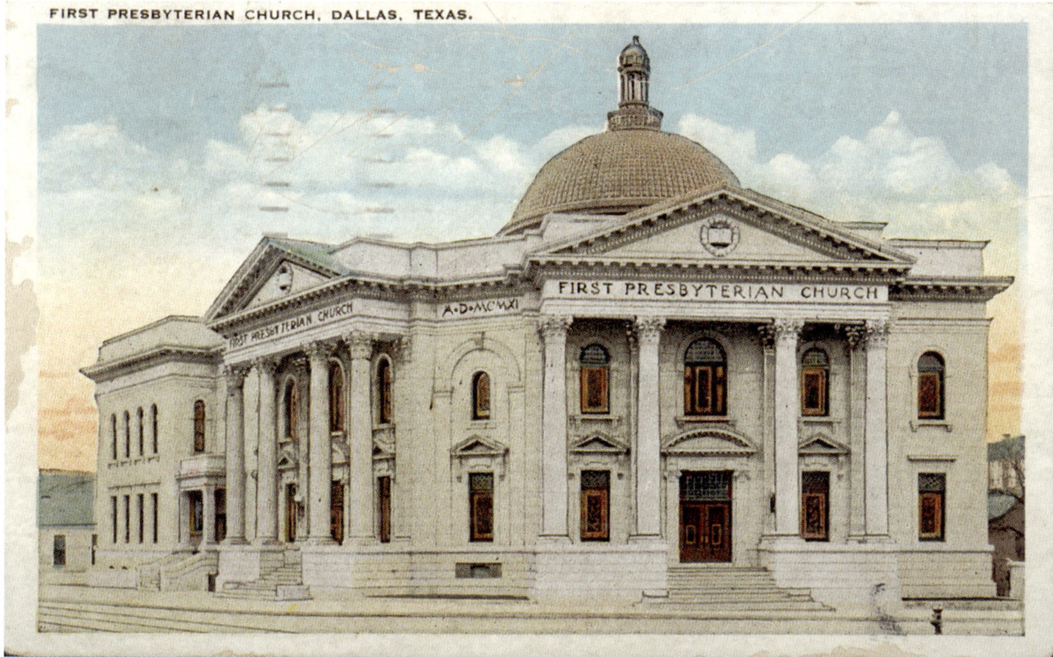

The First Presbyterian Church of Dallas was erected in 1856—they celebrated 150 years of service in 2006.

Cancelled 1952, $2-4

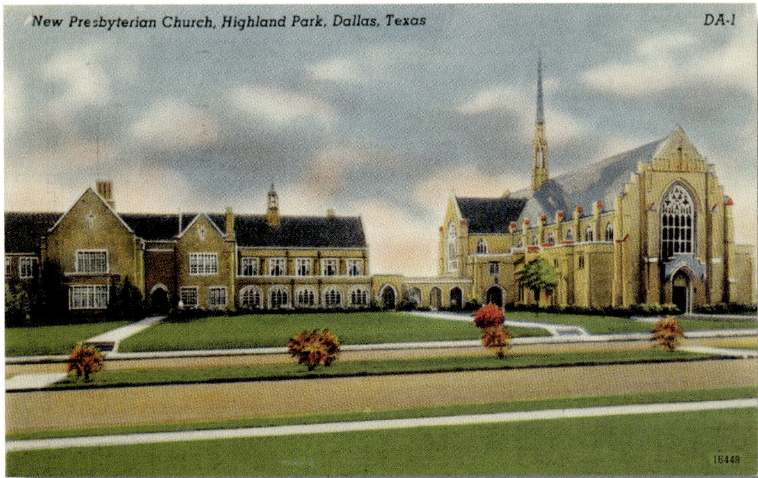

Since the early 1920s, the Highland Park Presbyterian Church has been welcoming worshipers to their church in University Park.

Cancelled 1952, $2-4

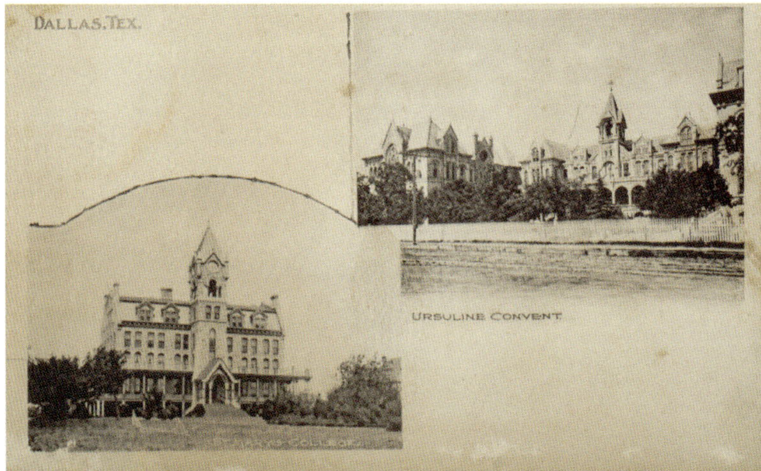

St. Mary's College and the Ursuline Convent. The Ursuline Convent is also known as the Ursuline Academy. This religious order was founded in Italy in 1535, with a mission to educate girls and to care for the sick and needy. St. Mary's College also caters to women and began construction in 1886. It was completed and opened in 1889.

Circa early 1900s, $6-8

Buildings

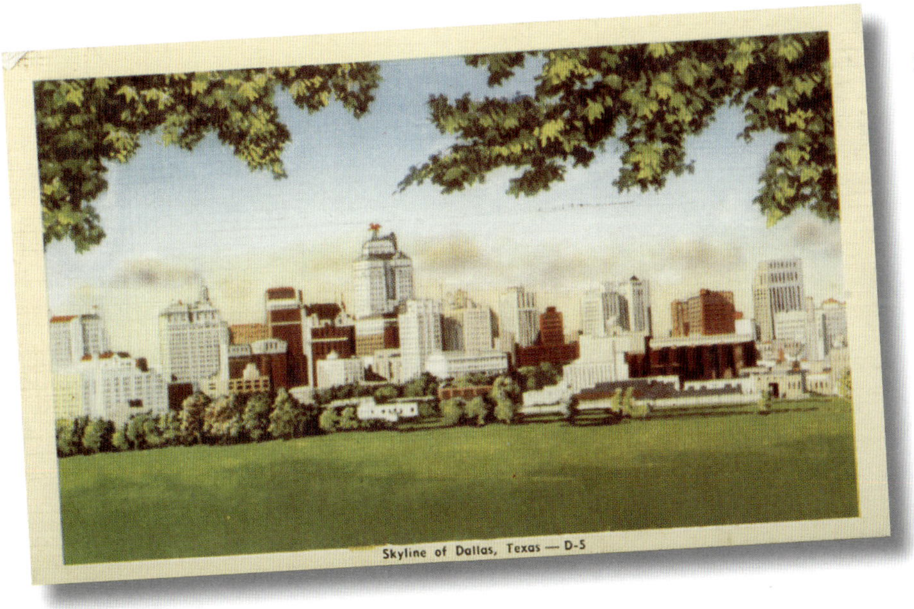

The buildings of Dallas provided many services for the citizens at the turn of the century, and we now find that this trend has been refurbished into services for those in today's world. Many of the buildings you will see here have been historically restored and have even been turned to for housing needs of the still-thriving Dallas population.

The skyline of Dallas, showing the magnificent skyscrapers and buildings.

Circa 1914, $2-4

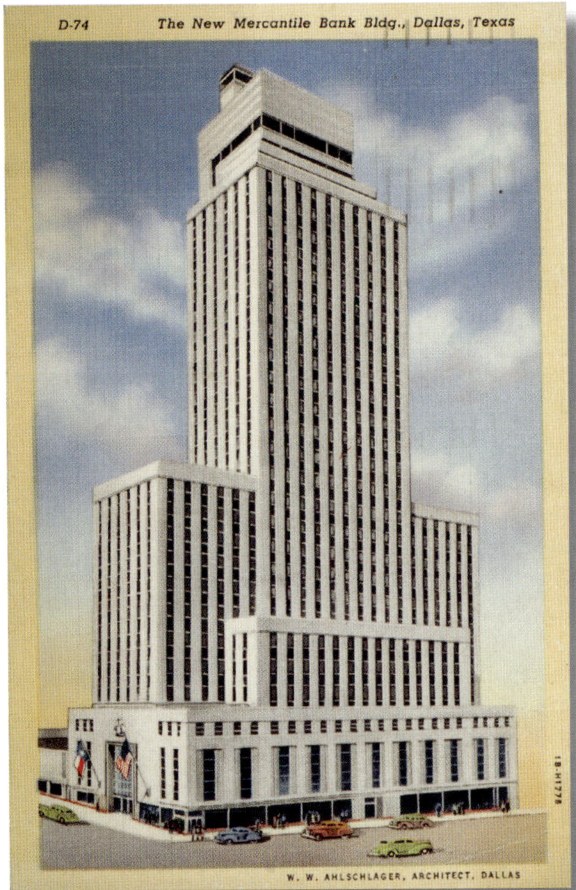

The Mercantile Bank Building, thirty stories high, was said to be one of the most modern (and largest) buildings west of the Mississippi. Construction for this high-rise building began in 1941. Prior to that, the post office was located on this site (from 1889 – 1930).

Cancelled 1943, $2-4

Once called the largest bank in Texas, the Republic Bank was founded by Eugene DeBogory in 1920. He promised that banking hours would be expanded to serve the working-class people.

Circa 1914, $2-4

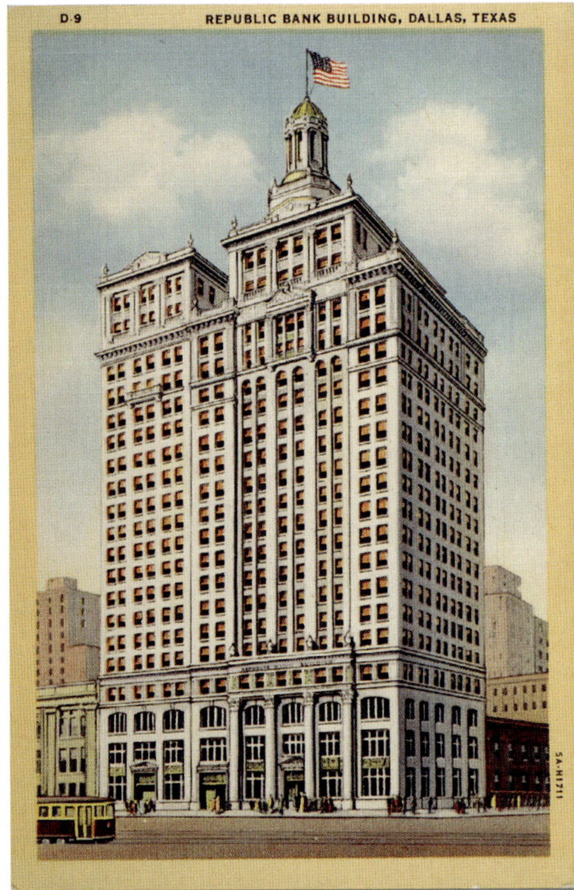

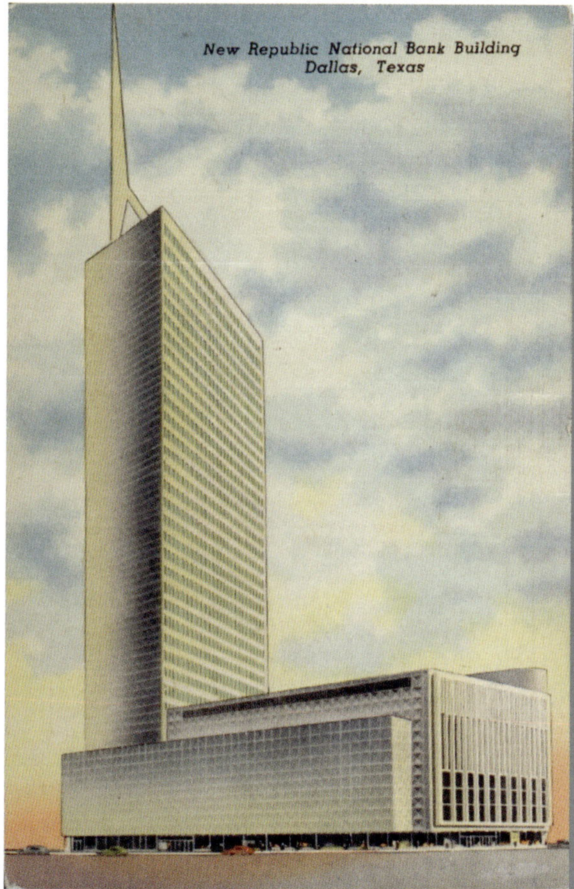

The Republic National Bank Building, thirty-six stories high, was the headquarters for the bank, which actually started, in 1920, as a the Guaranty Bank & Trust. The opening for this building was held at Fair Park with entertainment provided by the famous Bob Hope. Over 4,500 people attended.

Cancelled 1957, $4-6

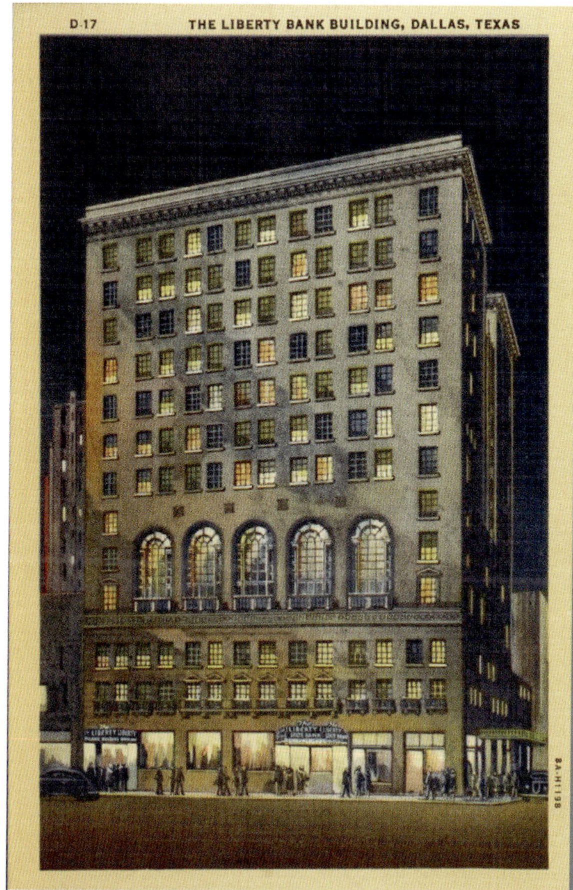

The Liberty Bank Building at night.

Circa 1914, $2-4

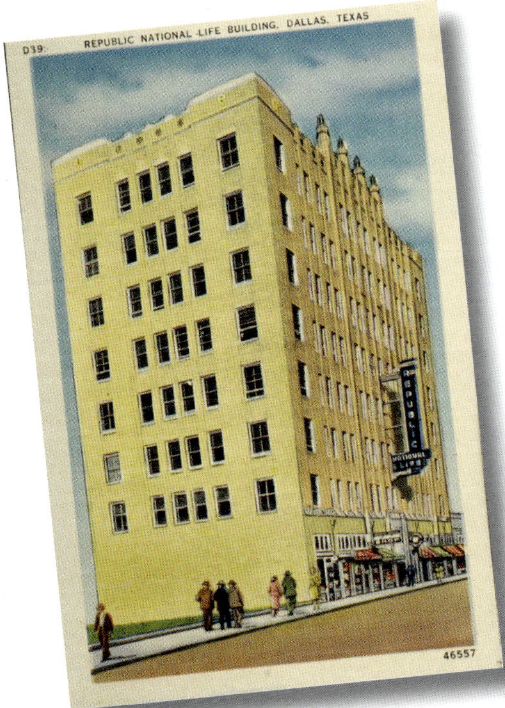

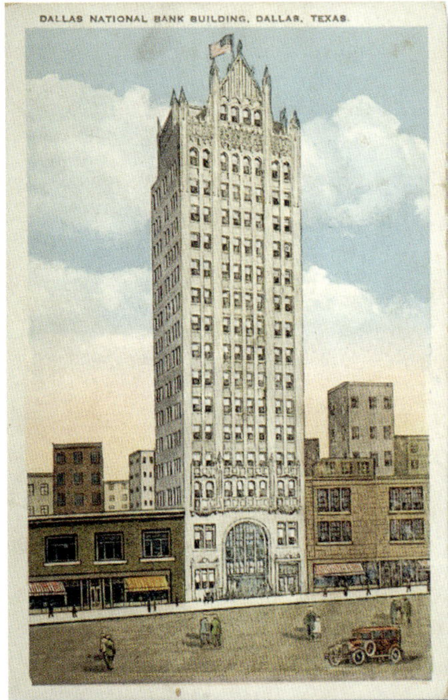

The Dallas National Bank Building is a 1920s era sky-rise building.

Cancelled 1931, $2-4

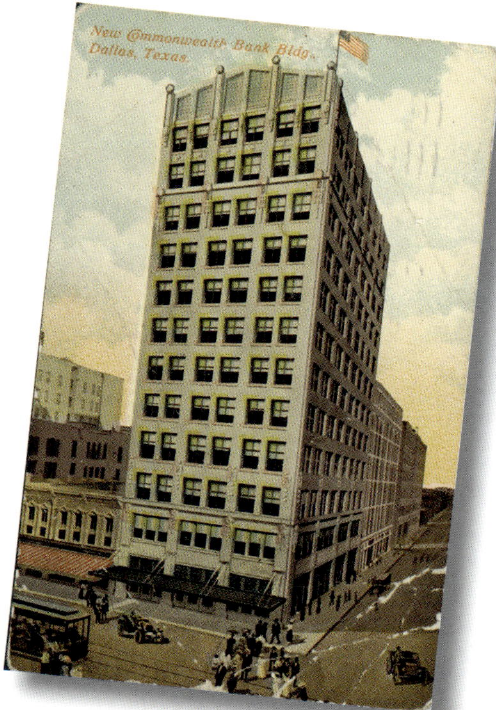

The Art Deco-style Republic National Life Building is now known as the Medical Dental Building and was constructed in 1925.

Circa 1914, $2-4

An early view of the Commonwealth Bank Building.

Cancelled 1913, $4-6

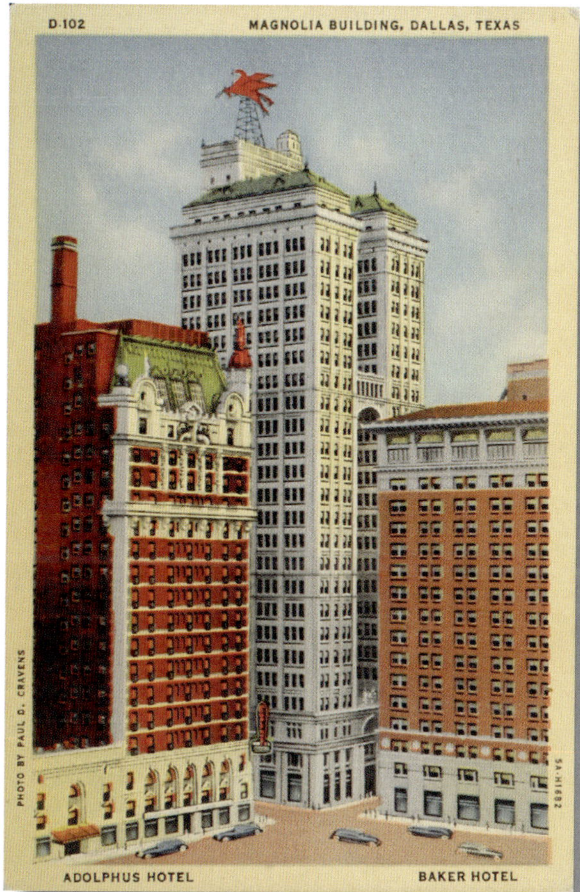

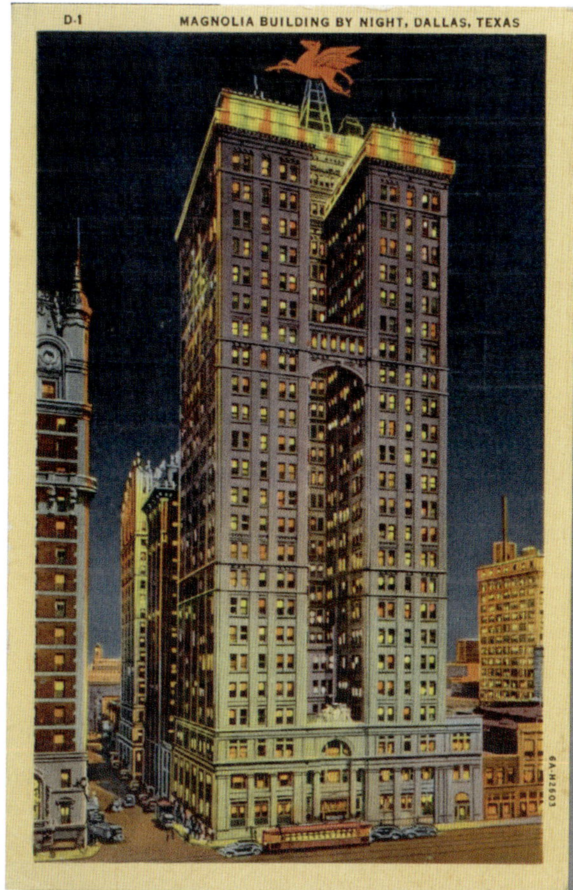

A 400-foot building with twenty-eight stories above ground and two beneath, The Magnolia Building has a revolving horse on top of the building that can be seen for miles. It is said to be a sign to help motorists navigate to downtown Dallas.

Circa 1947, $2-4 (left)
Cancelled 1943, $2-4 (right)

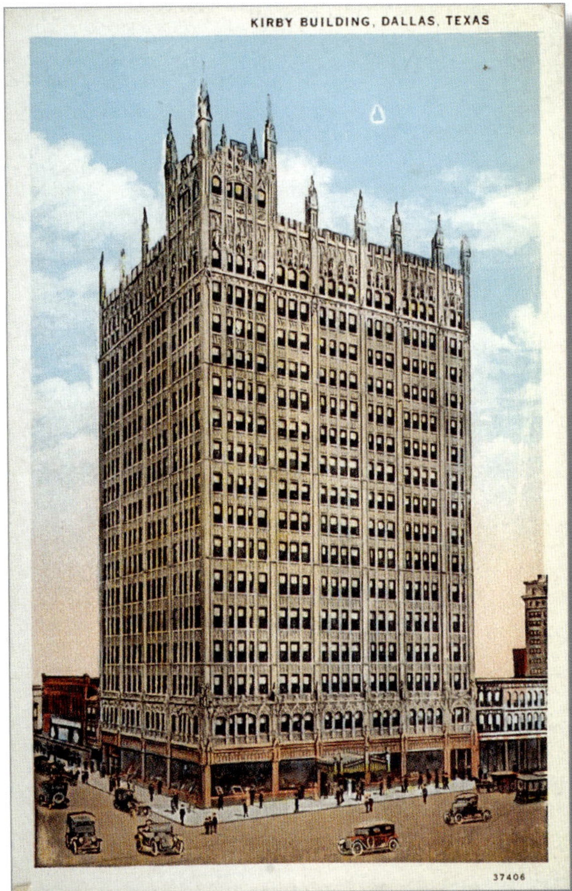

This seventeen-story Gothic building was only the second in the U.S. built in this style. The Kirby was originally built by Adolphus Busch to accompany the Adolphus Hotel.

Circa 1914, $2-4

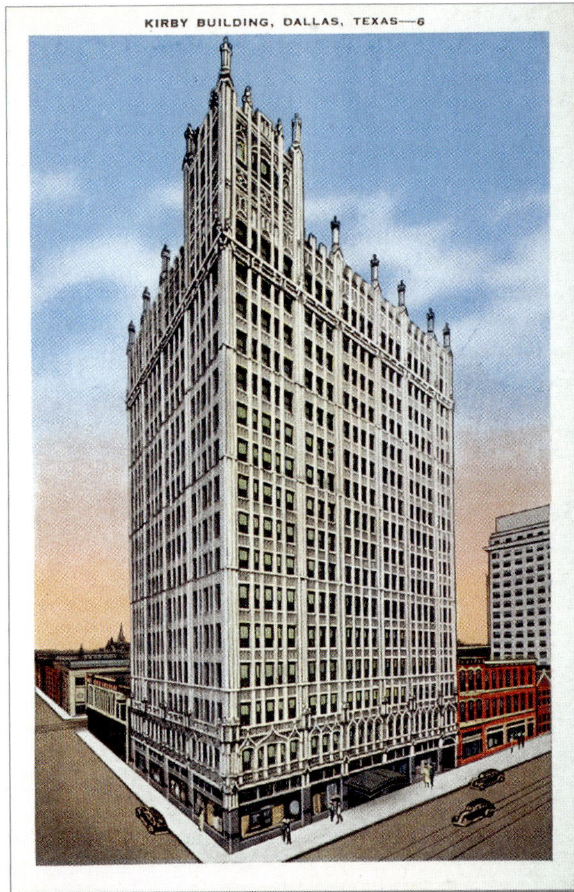

The building was originally named the Busch Building, but was renamed Kirby in 1918, when the Kirby Investment Group purchased it. Many people in Dallas nickname the Kirby, "the old girl."

Circa 1930s, $2-4

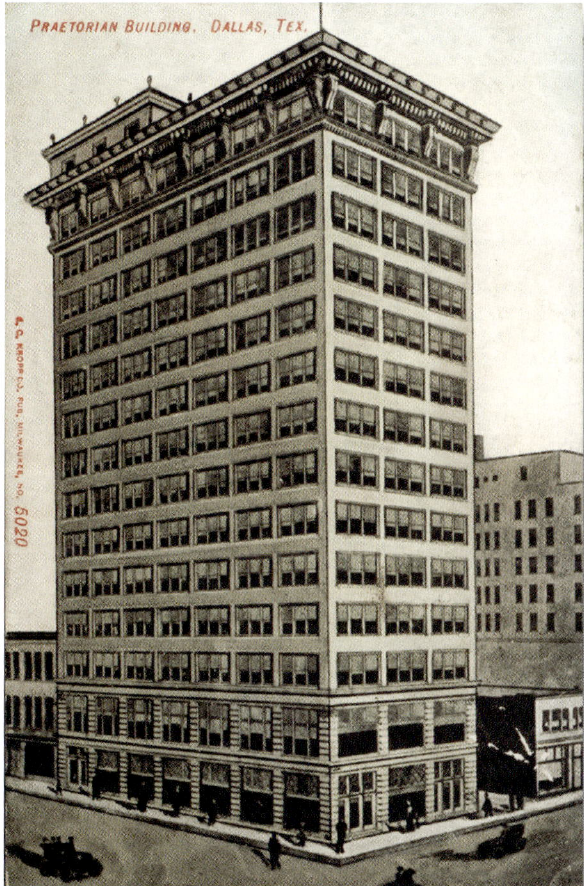

Built in 1909 for the Praetorian Order (an organization that's specialty was insurance), the Praetorian Building is a fourteen-story high-rise constructed in a neoclassical style.

Cancelled 1909, $6-8

Architect Mark Lemmon, born in Gainesville, was distinguished by varied historical revival building styles, such as the Tower Petroleum. Lemmon was also asked to design the Museum of Natural History in 1935, and the Hall of State in 1935.

Cancelled 1933, $2-4

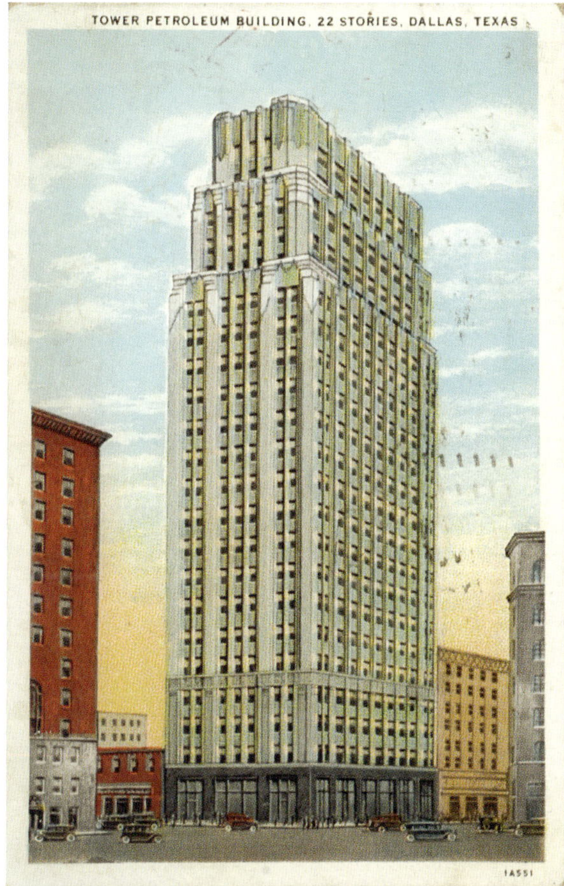

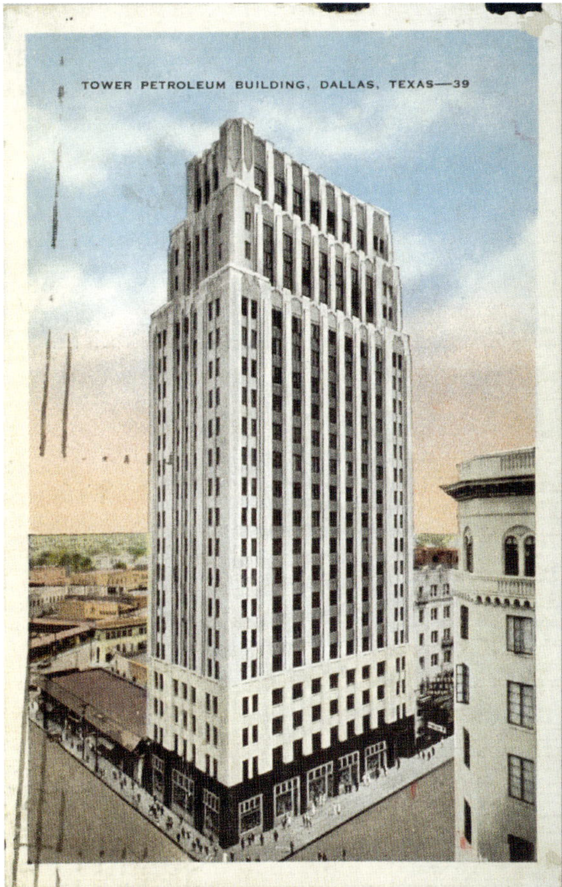

Designed in 1930, the Tower Petroleum Building was built as a twenty-two story high-rise.

Cancelled 1936, $2-4

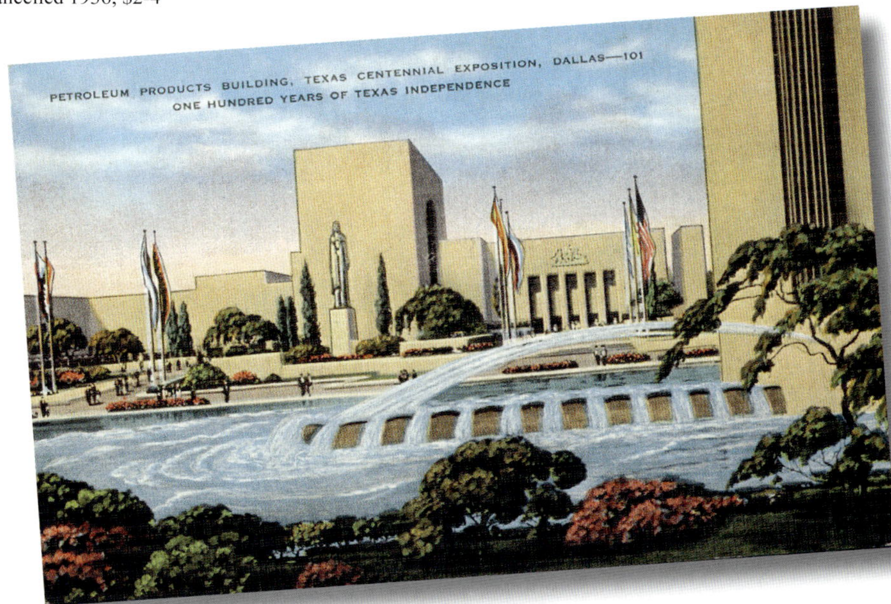

The Petroleum Products Building at the Texas Centennial was designed to be a permanent structure devoted to the exhibitions relating to oil. It cost approximately $500,000 to build this 35,000 square foot building.

Circa 1914, $2-4

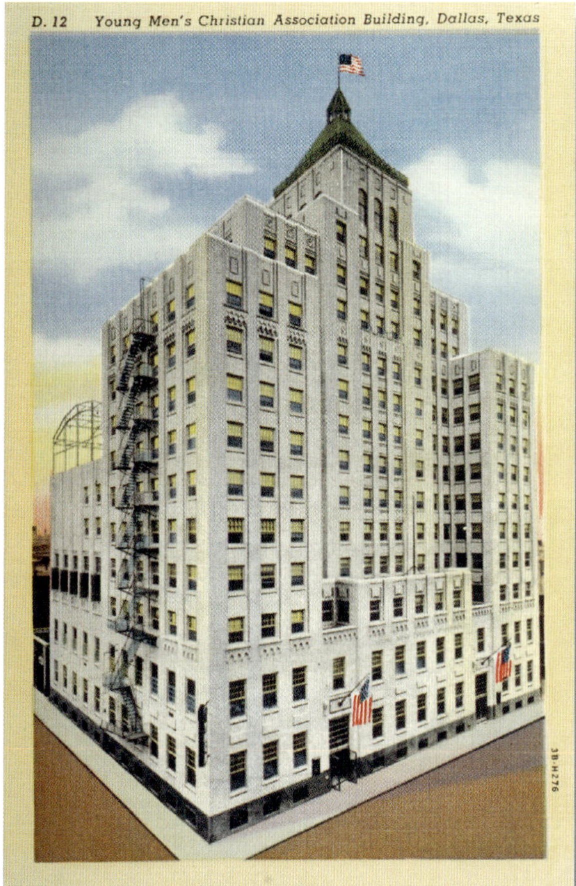

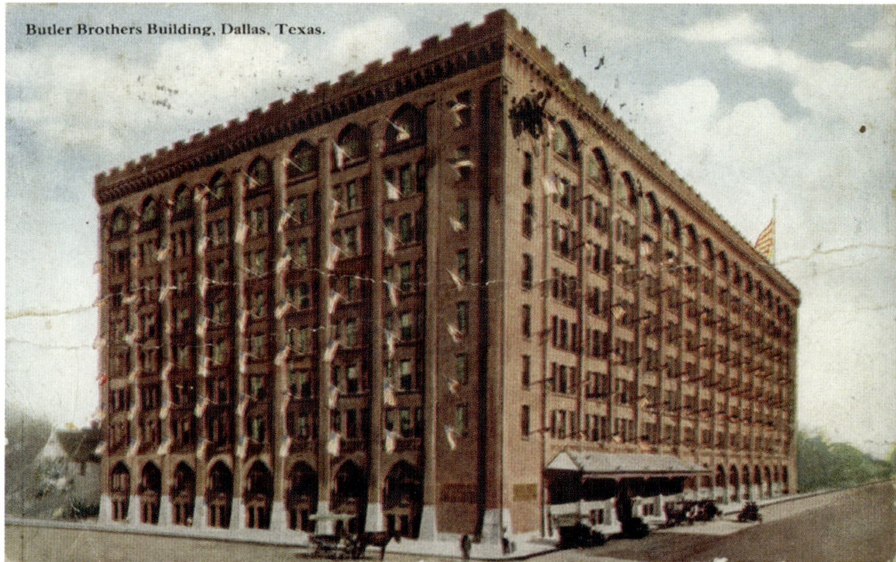

The Butler Brothers Building was built by Butler Brothers—a Chicago wholesaler—as their warehouse for the entire Southwest. Though it served Butler Brothers customers, eventually, it came to serve as a warehouse for another of their properties, the Ben Franklin Stores.

Cancelled 1916, $2-4

In 1931, the downtown YMCA was completed. The 15-story, 250-room building provided community outreach patterned after other successful centers and the Y's overall mission.

Circa 1914, $2-4

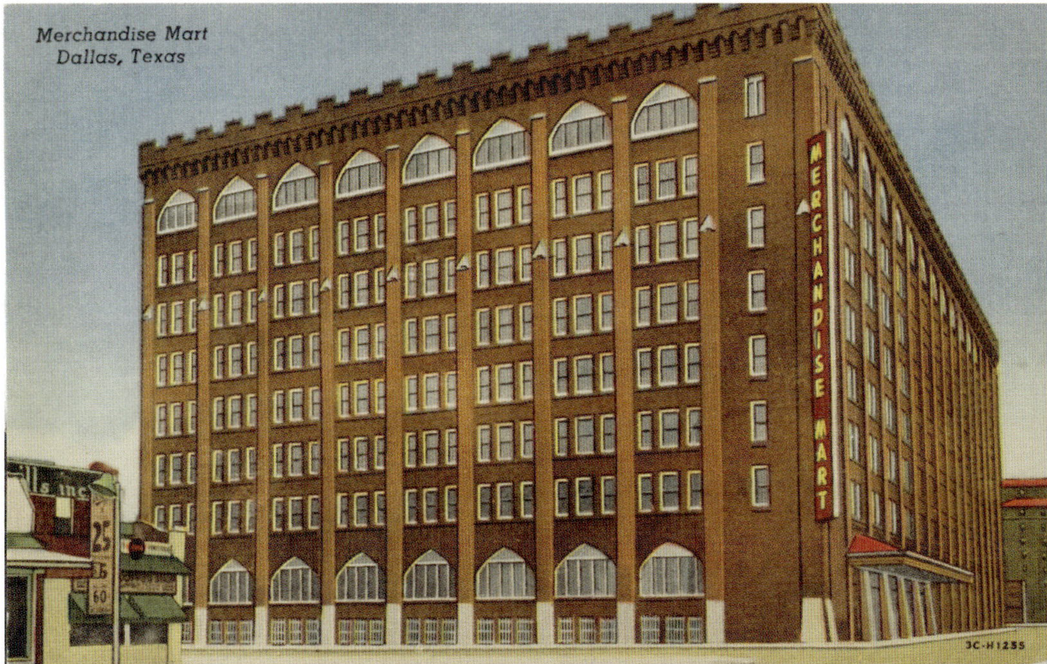

Upon expanding in 1917 and once more in 1932, the Butler Brothers Building was renamed Merchandise Mart of the Southwest.

Circa 1930s, $2-4

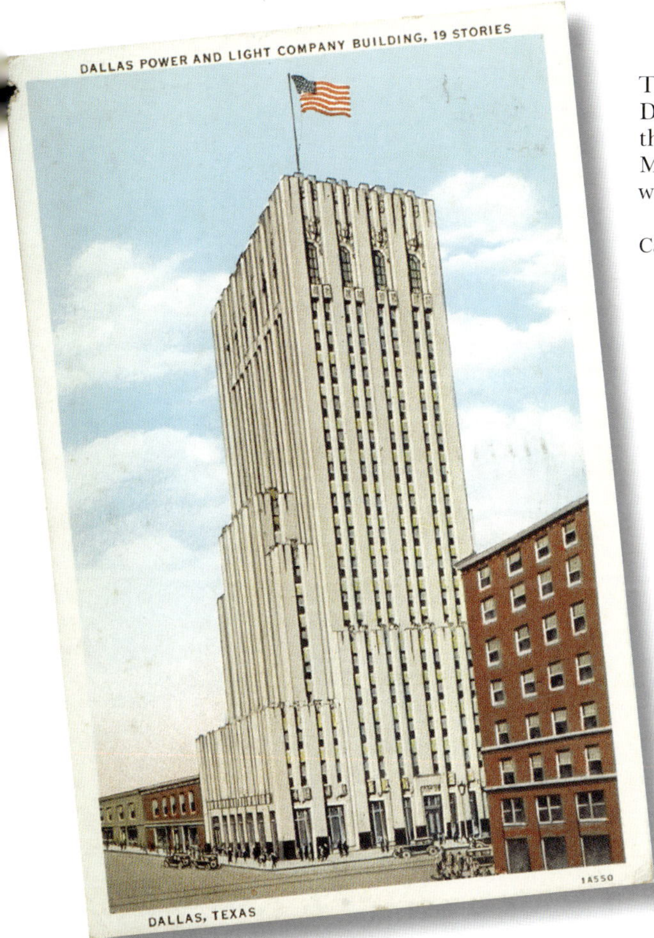

The eighteen-story Art Deco Dallas Power and Light was the first building west of the Mississippi to be electrically welded.

Cancelled 1938, $2-4

Also known as Texas Utilities (TXU), the Dallas Power and Light Company was built by Gardner & Howe Engineers and C. L. Shaw & Company in 1931.

Cancelled 1949, $2-4

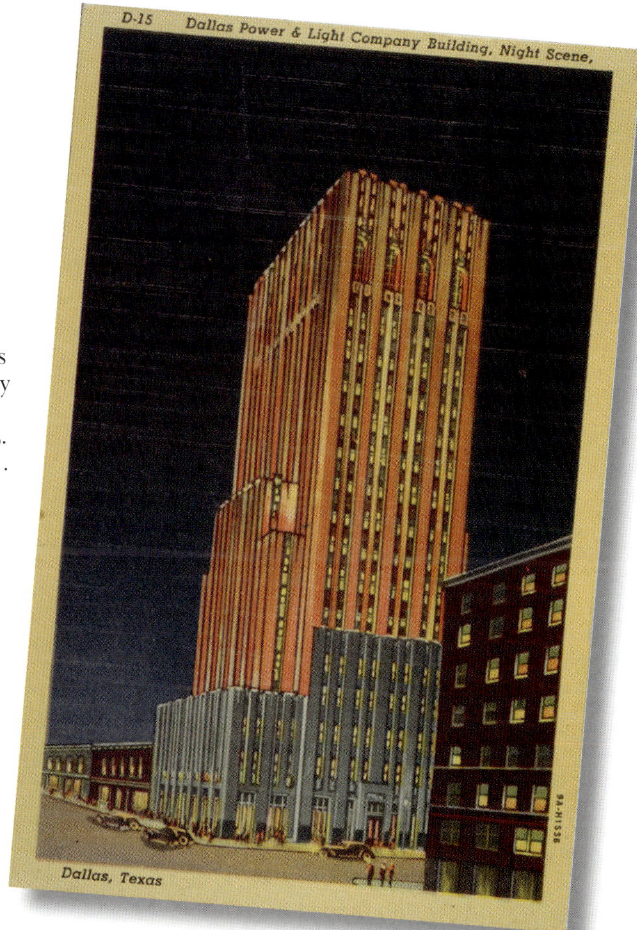

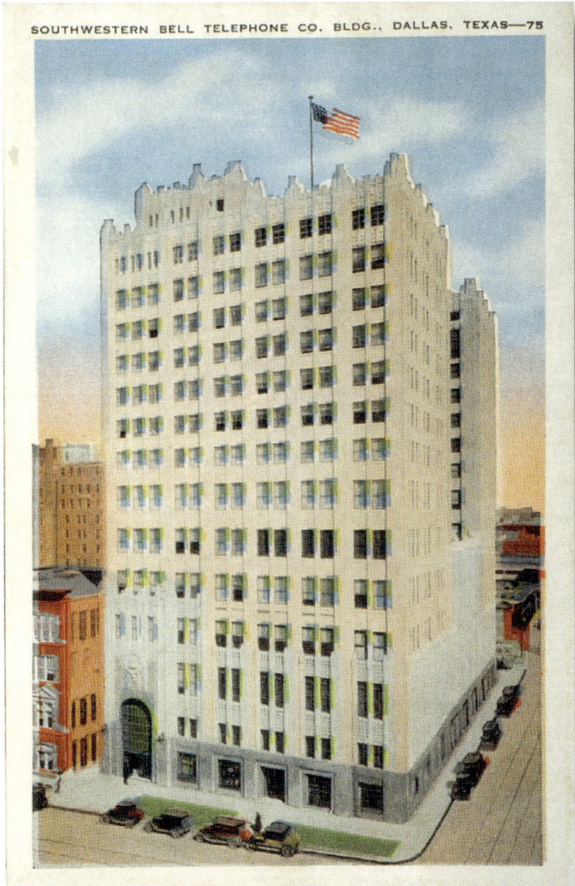

The Southwestern Bell Telephone Company Building.

Circa 1920s, $2-4

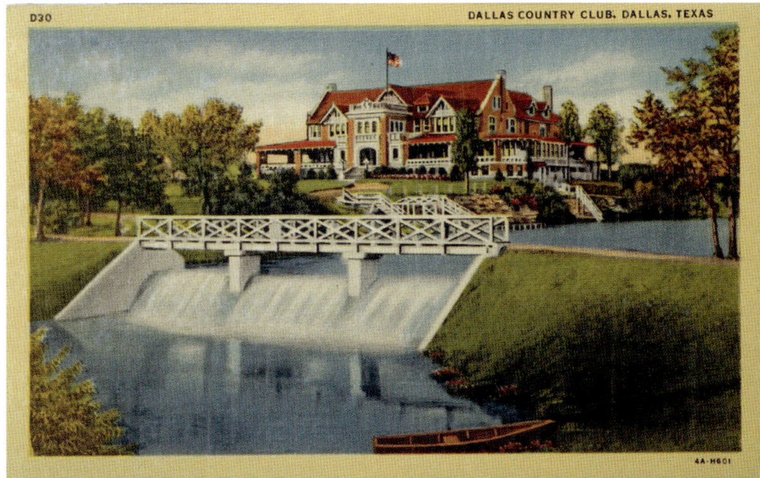

The Dallas Country Club was founded in 1896 and is a "*traditional, private, full service, family oriented social club dedicated to providing members superior services, programs, staff and facilities in a cost effective and business-like manner.*"

Circa 1914, $2-4

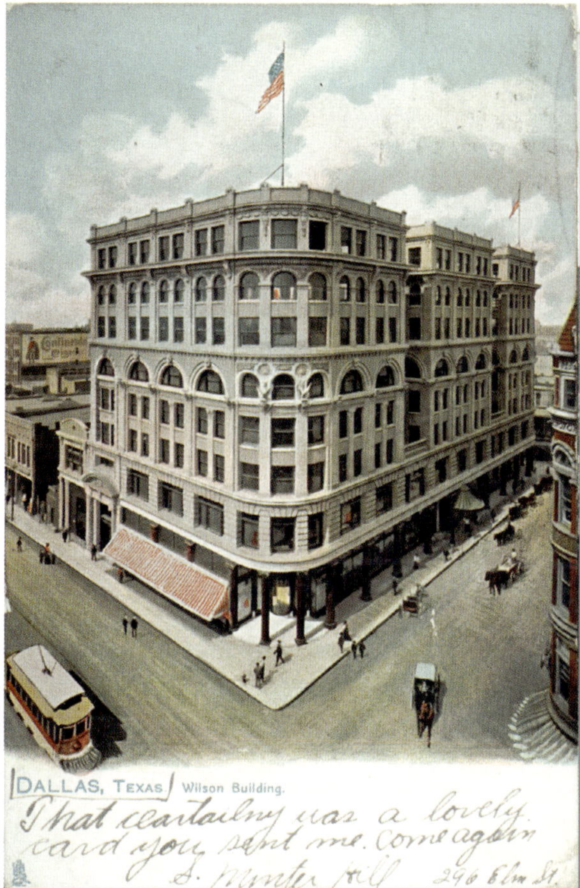

TheWilson Building was built by the wealthy Dallas cattleman, J. B. Wilson in 1903. The first eight-story building in the state, it originally housed the Titche-Goettinger Department Store on the first floor, while the upper floors held offices.

Cancelled 1907, $6-8

Sanguinet & Staats, in 1911, built a twelve-story annex to the Wilson Building. The main tenant, after 1929, was H. L. Green's Department Store (also known as a "poor man's Neiman Marcus").

Circa early 1900s, $4-6

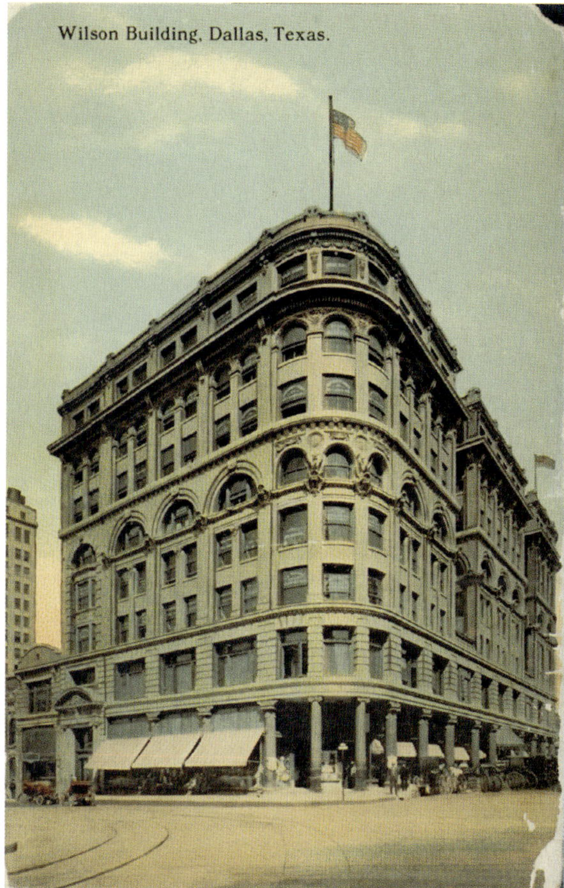

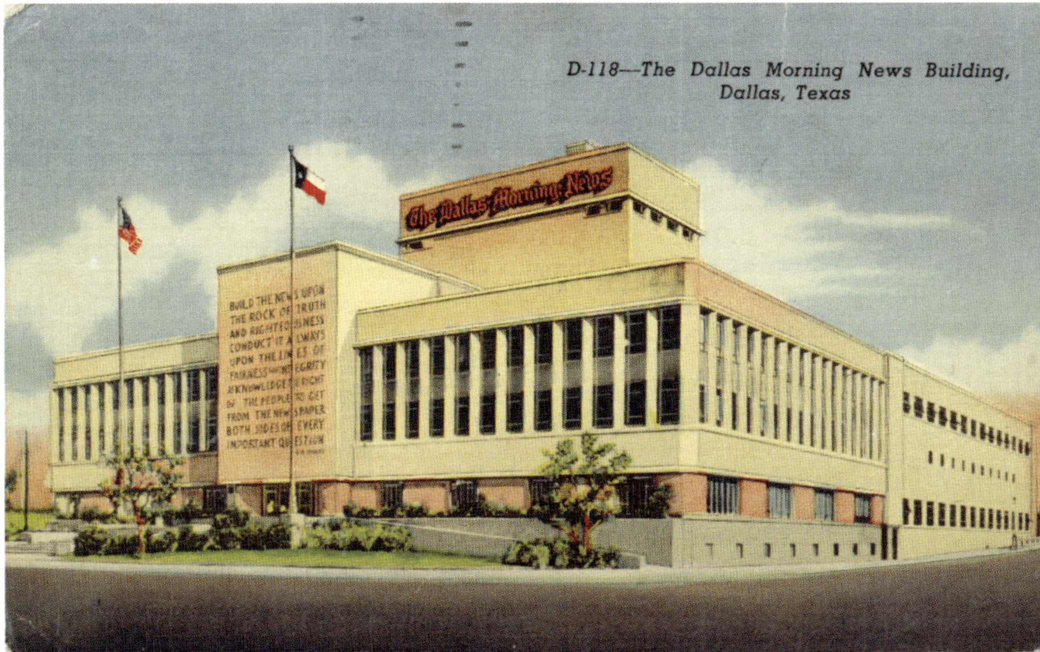

First published in 1885 with a circulation of 5,000, The Dallas Morning News was providing news to other North Texas cities by using the rails. An eight to twelve-page daily edition (with sixteen pages on Sunday!) was being printed by 1888.

Cancelled 1958, $2-4

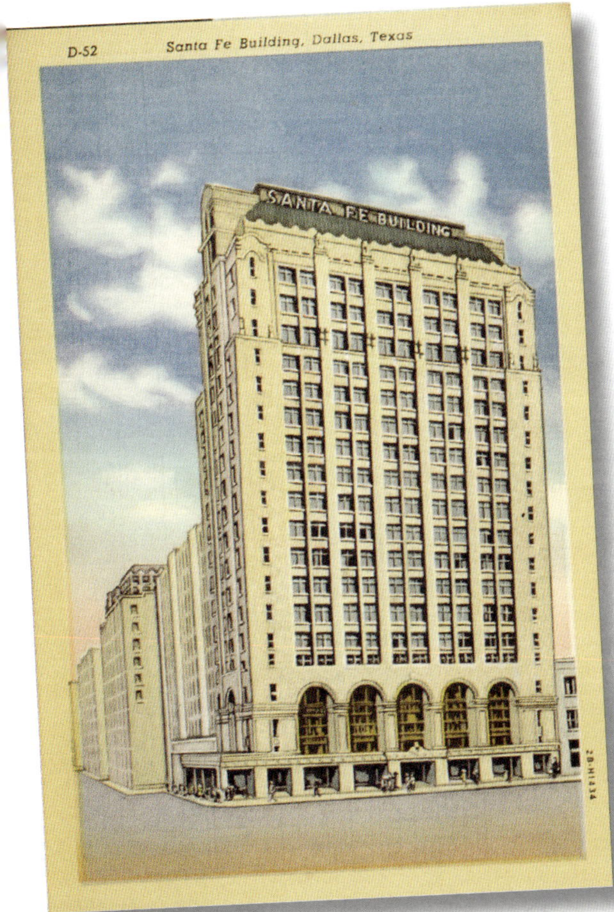

Though the Santa Fe Building was to be demolished in 1987, it was spared, and two of the four-buildings in the complex were listed in the National Register of Historic Places in 1997. Now only buildings one, two, and four remain.

Cancelled 1925, $2-4

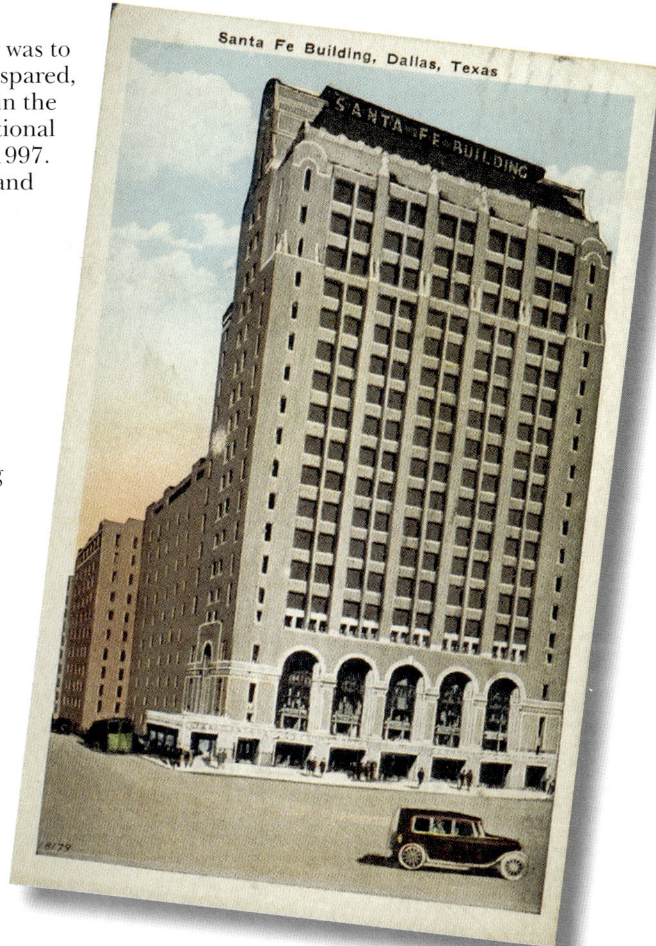

The Santa Fe Building, built in a quasi-Spanish Renaissance style, provided multifaceted usage for warehousing as well as the provision of offices for the Gulf, Colorado & Santa Fe Railroad system. There were tunnels beneath connecting a four-building complex—with the availability for trains to enter the multiplex.

Circa 1914, $2-4

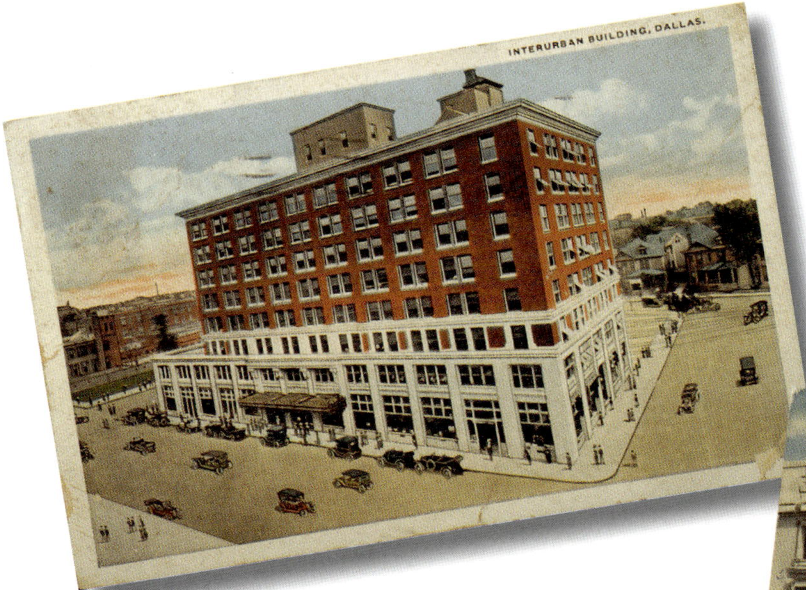

Built in 1916 as a nine-story building able to accommodate thirty-five inter-urban trains at any given time, the Interurban Building was first named the Dallas Interurban Terminal Building, and later, Continental Trailways.

Cancelled 1919, $2-4

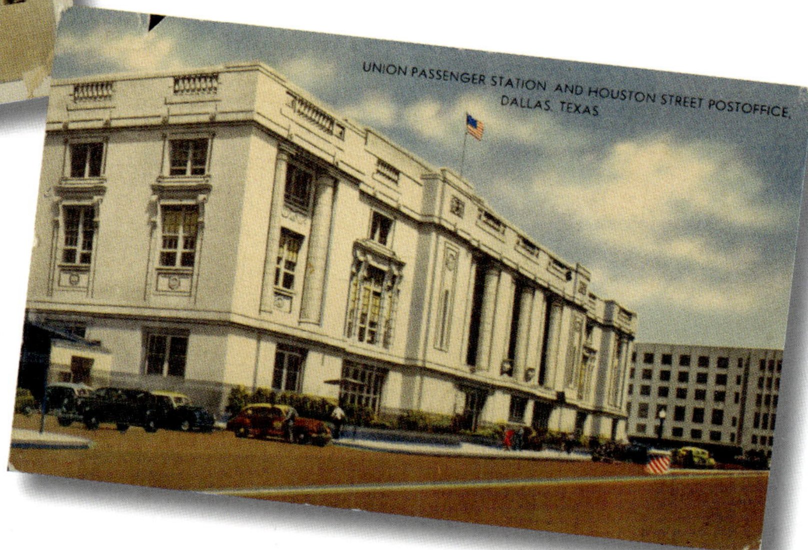

The Union Station was built in 1916 to merge five railroad stations spread around Dallas. In this way, the one facility served as a major transportation hub for the Southwest. As many as eighty trains were known to stop at the station during the station's peak years.

Cancelled 1946, $2-4

Hotels

Dallas has been hostess to travelers within its flourishing city limits from the very beginning. Lodging that displays all the luxury of the times are depicted in the following scenes, ranging from splendid locations for night life, entertainment, and recreation, to the quick and comfy styles embraced by hotels catering to the business traveler. Whether looking at the historic charm of the Adolphus or the magnificence of the Statler Hilton, one thing is certain: Dallas has a welcoming way about her that will continue to build her tourism through the ages.

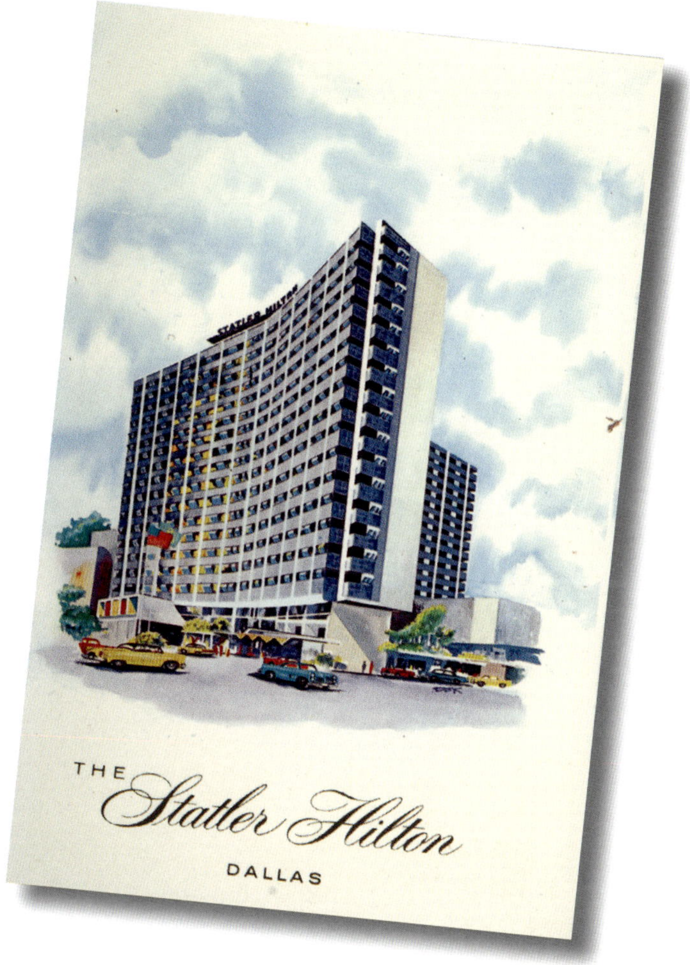

The Statler Hilton was a Y-shaped building housing 1001 rooms and was equipped with air conditioning, a rooftop sundeck, and heliport.

Circa 1950s, $2-4

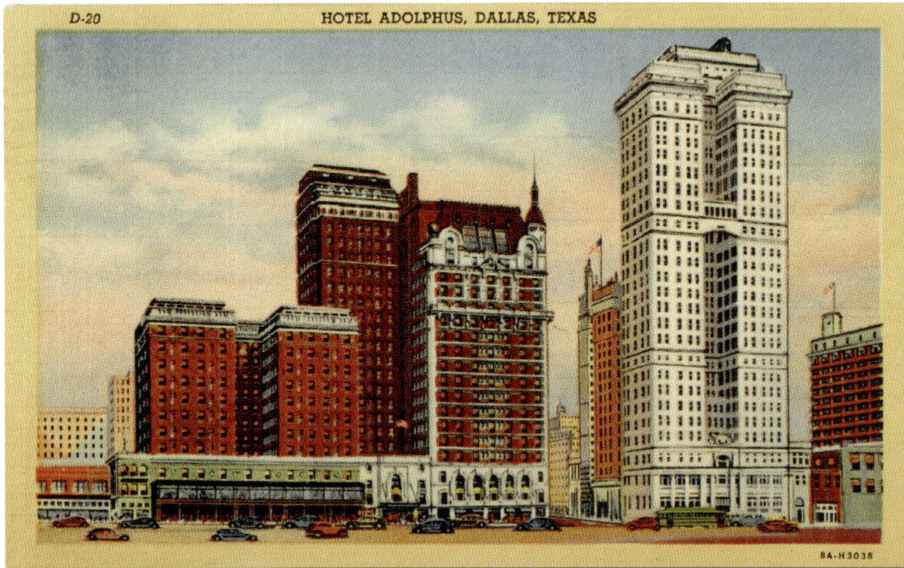

The Hotel Adolphus claimed to be the largest hotel in Dallas and is located in the business district. It was especially known for the popular Century Room.

Cancelled 1951, $2-4

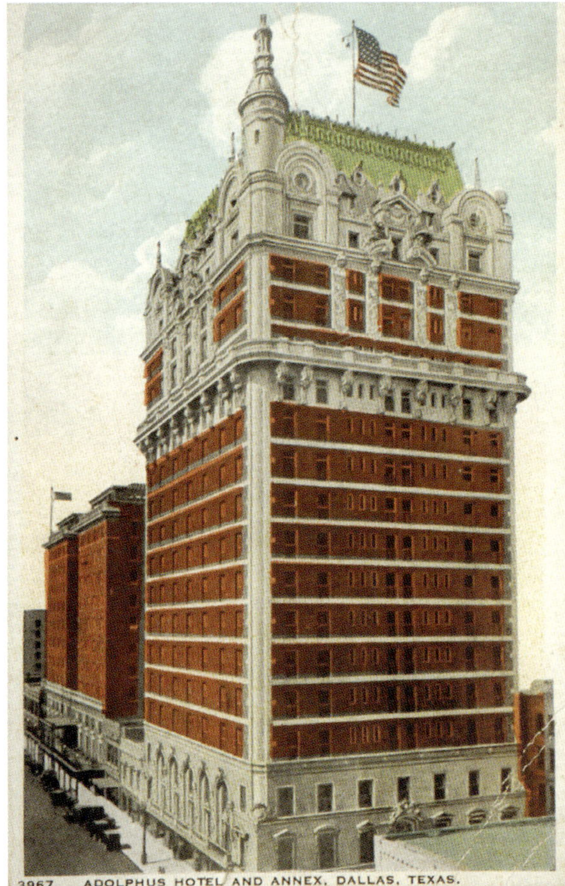

One could get an air-conditioned room with bath for rates beginning at $2.50 per day at the Hotel Adolphus.

Circa early 1900s, $6-8

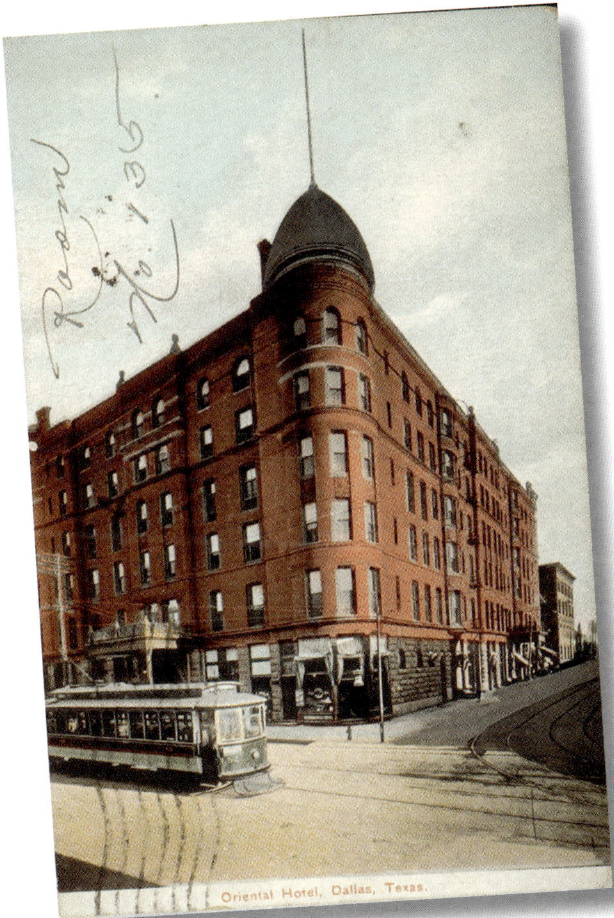

Thomas William Field, a premier real estate developer and builder started the Oriental Hotel project (often called "Field's Folly" because of its $500,000 price tag) in 1893, projected as the "most elegant hotel east of the Mississippi."

Cancelled 1909, $4-6

At the corner of Akard and Commerce, the hotel provided 150 rooms with lobbies, bars, and dining rooms decorated with Italian marble and mahogany.

Circa early 1900s, $14-16

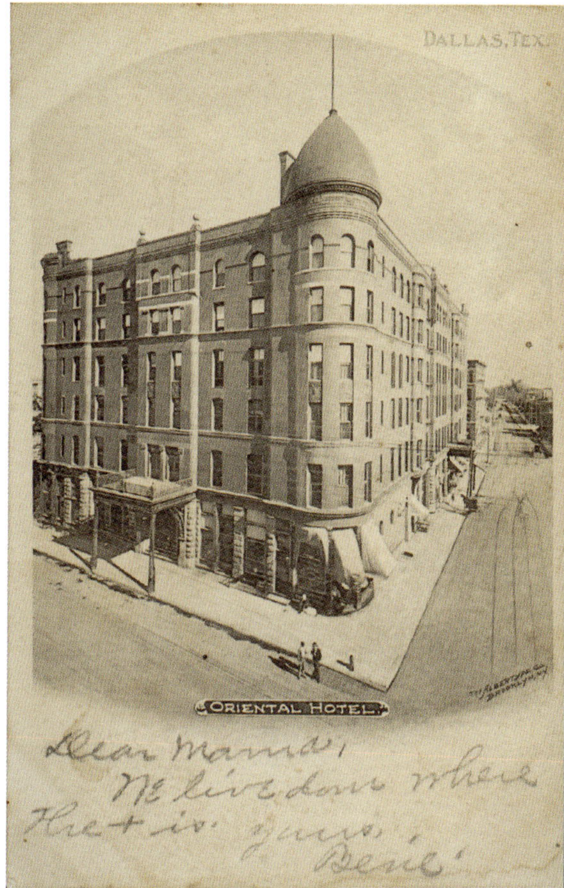

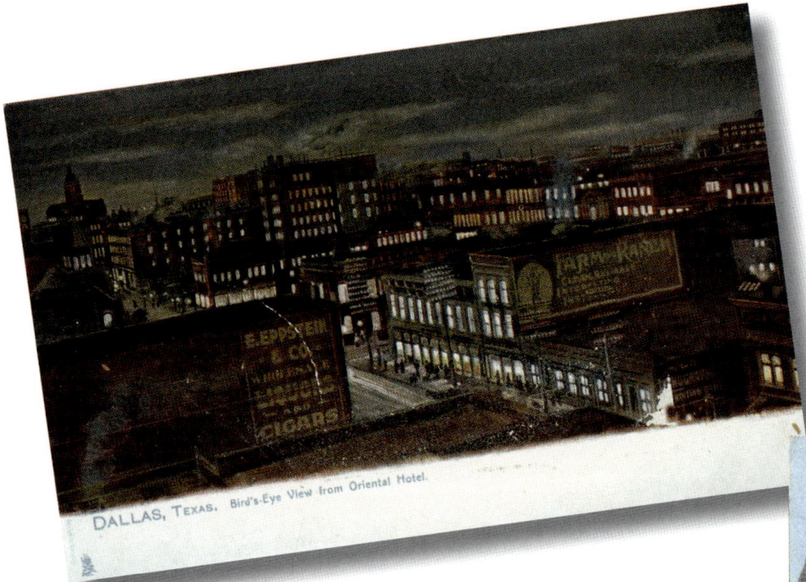

The view from the Oriental Hotel. The hotel was sold to a group of businessmen from St. Louis during bankruptcy proceedings.

Circa early 1900s, $8-10

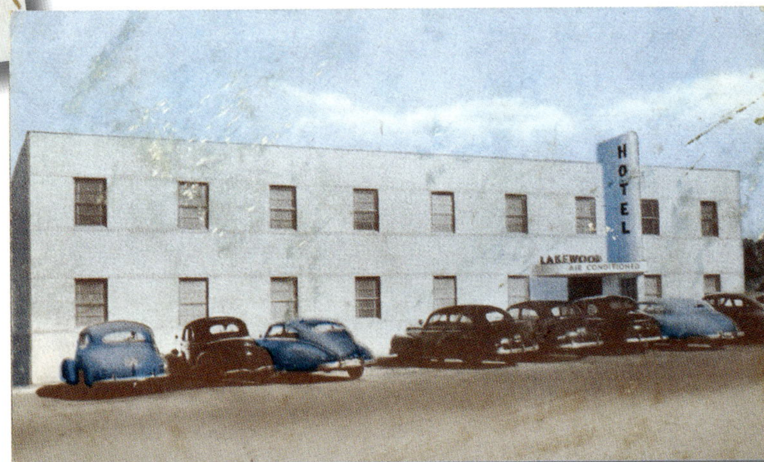

The Lakewood Hotel was known as a suburban hotel—comfortable and tastefully decorated. Located in the Lakewood Shopping Village, this hotel was less than fifteen minutes from downtown Dallas.

Circa 1940s, $2-4

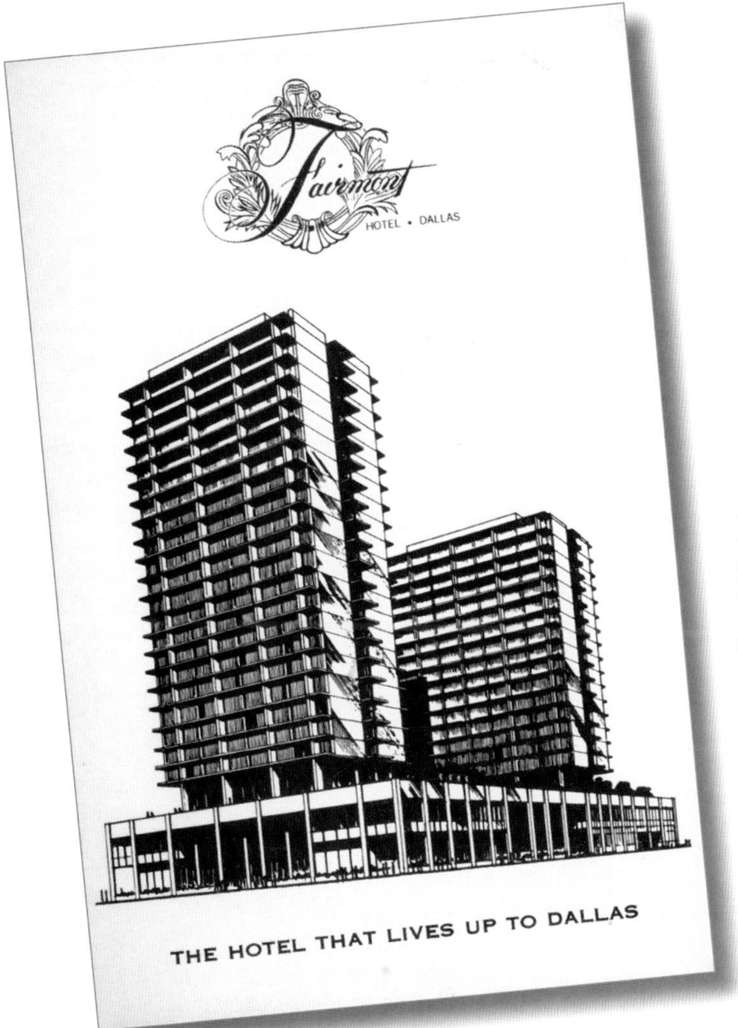

A more recent hotel, The Fairmont Dallas, opening in 1969, was noted as a luxury hotel and also the tallest building in the city. It is located in the "Arts District."

Circa 1960s, $2-4

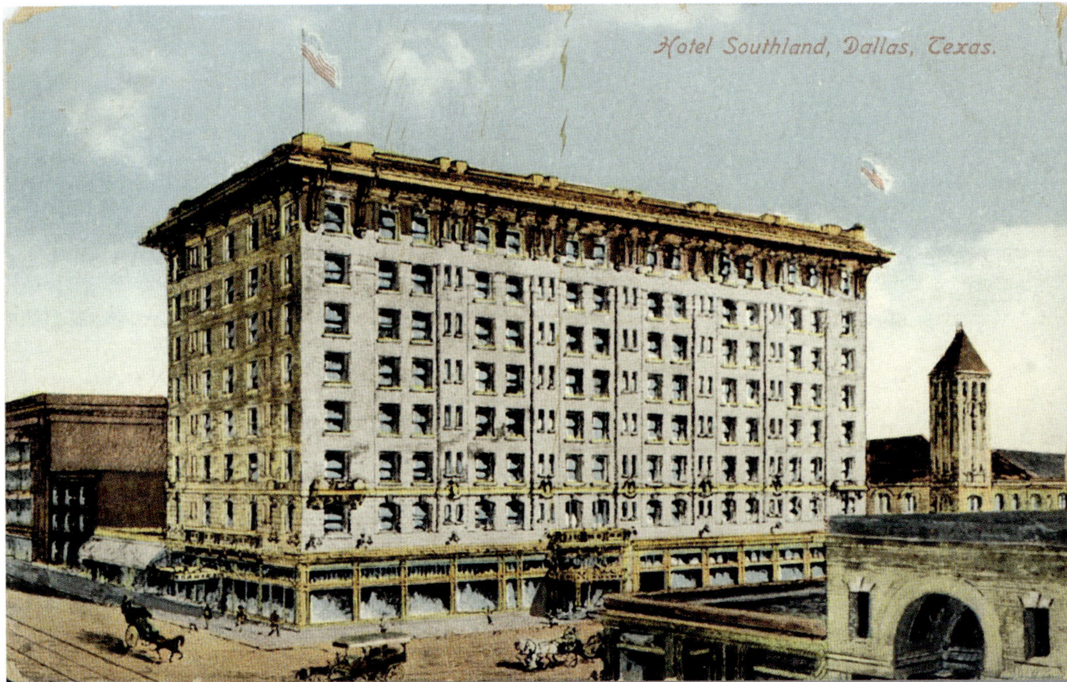

Erected at the corner of Main and Murphy in 1907, the Hotel Southland was a 116- foot high-rise designed by architects Parkinson and Bergstrom. (The hotel has been demolished.)

Circa 1907, $4-6

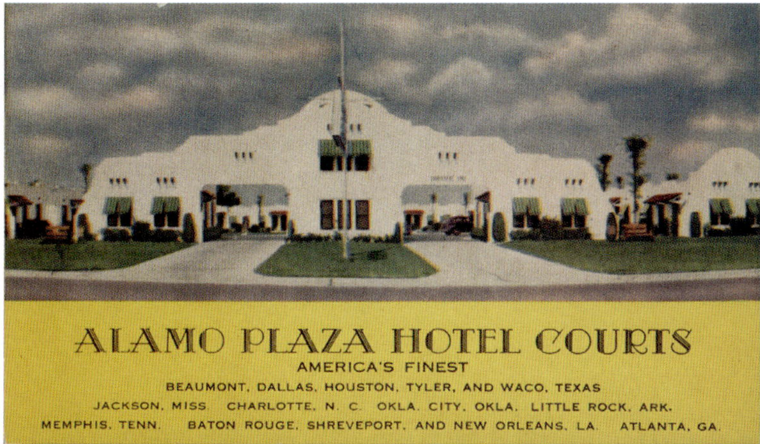

The Alamo Plaza Hotel Courts was part of a chain of "clean, well-maintained, well-organized, comfortable, and respectable motels" in Texas, including Dallas. The chain was developed by early motel developer Edgar Lee Torrance, beginning in Waco in 1929, and using the Alamo as a design tool.

Circa 1940s, $2-4

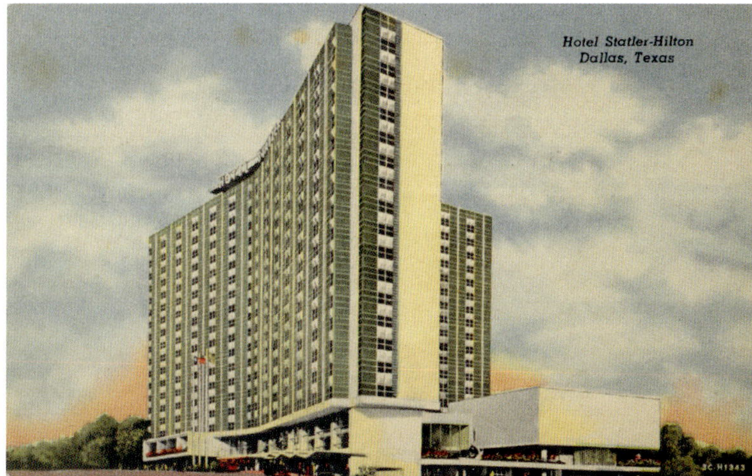

Ellsworth Statler founded the Statler Hotel chain, but the Dallas Statler was not built until after his death (1928). Erected in 1956, the Statler-Hilton was closed in 2001 to await a new owner.

Circa 1920s, $2-4

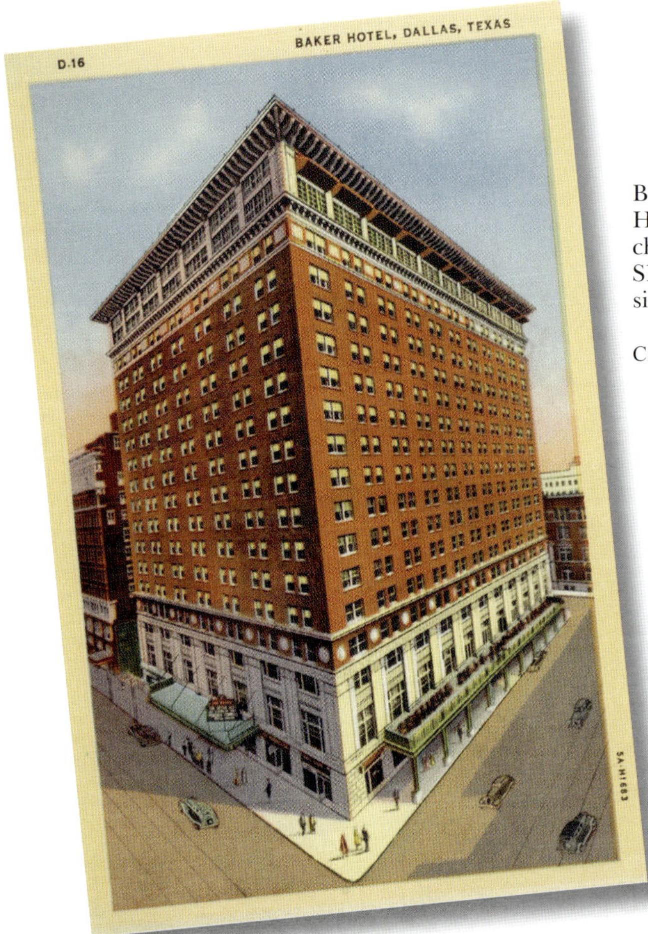

Built in 1925, the eighteen-story Baker Hotel was demolished as part of a synchronized building demolition. The One SBC Plaza (covering an entire block) now sits at the location (built in 1984).

Circa 1930s, $2-4

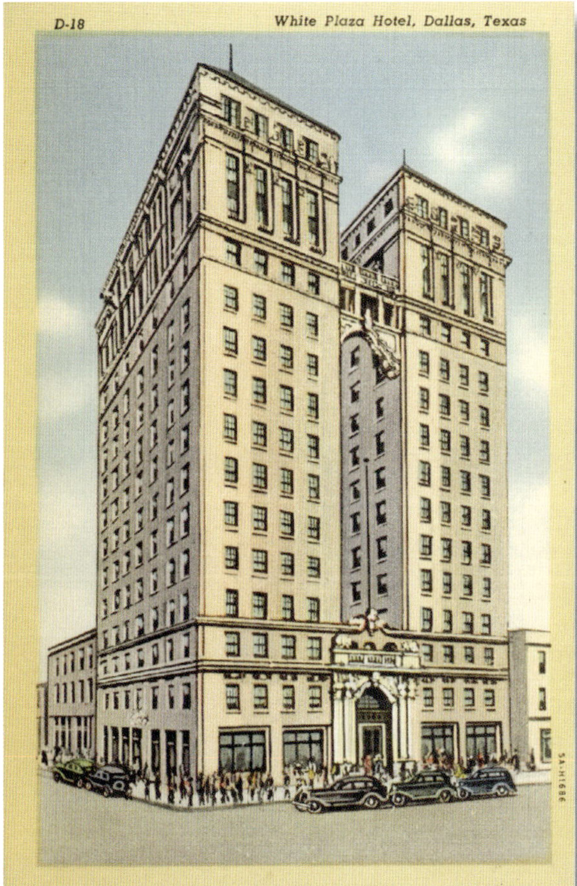

Located on Main Street, the White Plaza Hotel (usually called "The Plaza Hotel") was erected in 1925 in a Beaux-arts style. Conrad Hilton was the founder of the Hilton Hotel chain, making this Dallas lodging the second in his procession of hotels.

Circa 1930s, $2-4

A lovely historic building, Cliff Towers Hotel is located across the Trinity River with a view of the downtown area. Though it began as a hotel, later it became a nursing home. Developers have had plans over the years for renovations, but according to radio station KBOX (2006), this twelve-story building remains vacant.

Circa 1914, $2-4

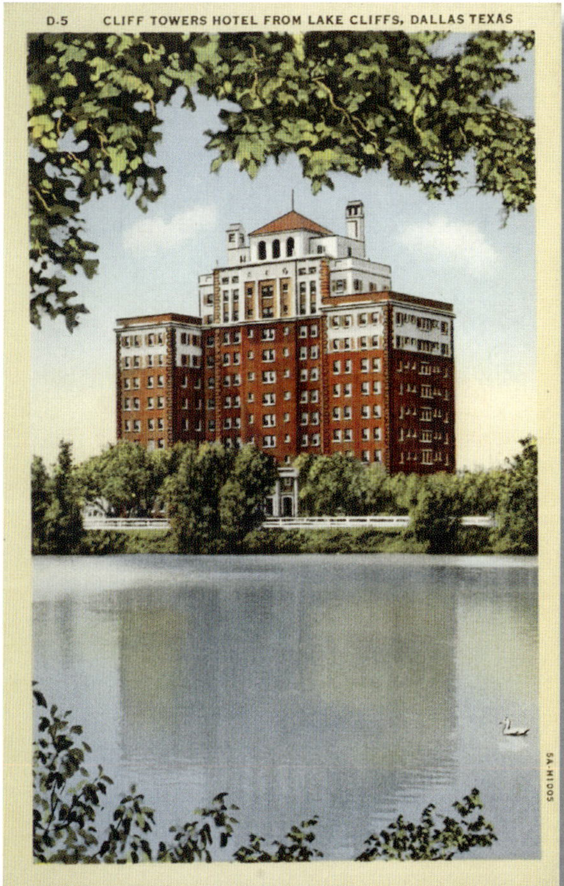

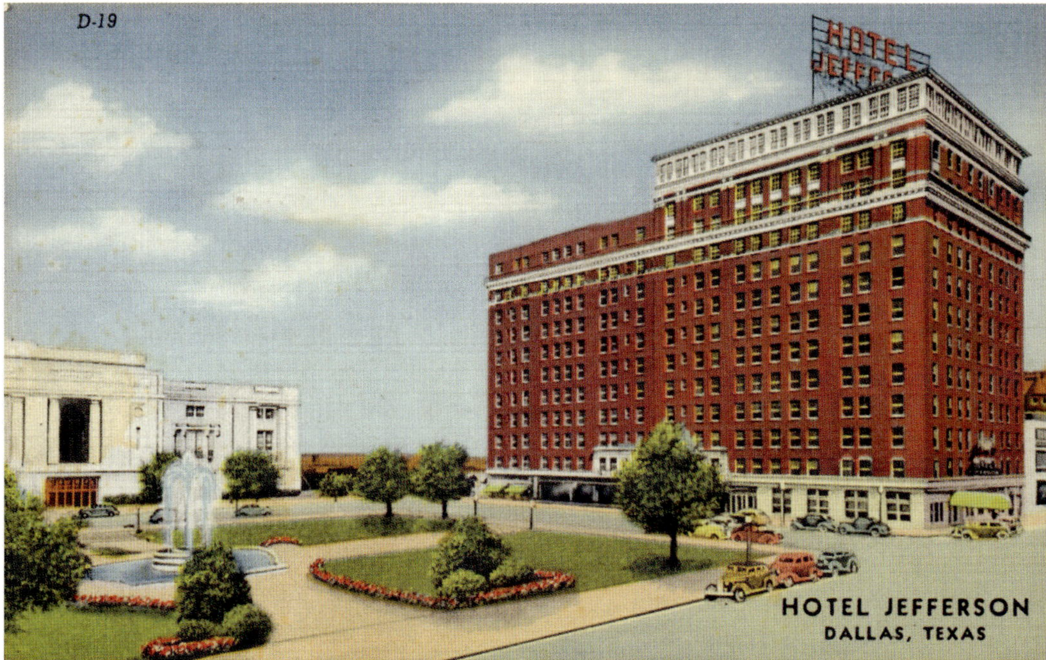

Built in 1927, this thirteen-story high-rise building has been demolished. At one point, the hotel was known as the Hotel Lawrence.

Circa 1930s, $2-4

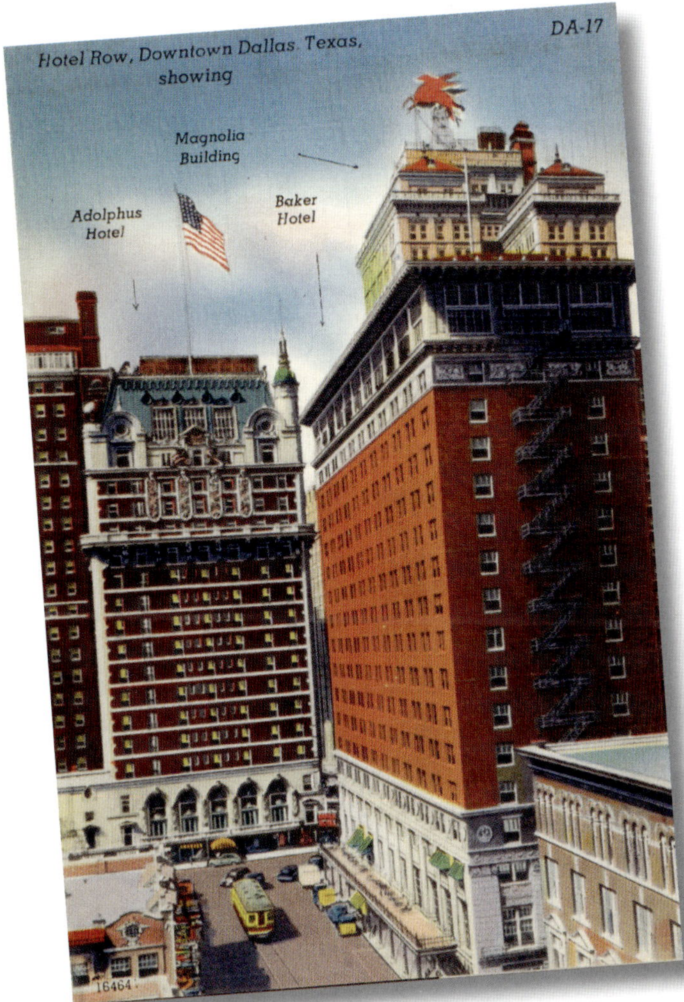

A view of hotel row in Dallas.

Circa 1930s, $4-6

The Streets of Dallas

The streets of Dallas have been bustling from its first historic founding to the varied scenes shown here in wide-ranging times and places. Shopping, working, sight-seeing, and entertaining have all been important to residents and visitors of this fair city. And the streets clearly symbolize the importance of forward-thinking, planning, and executing economic presence.

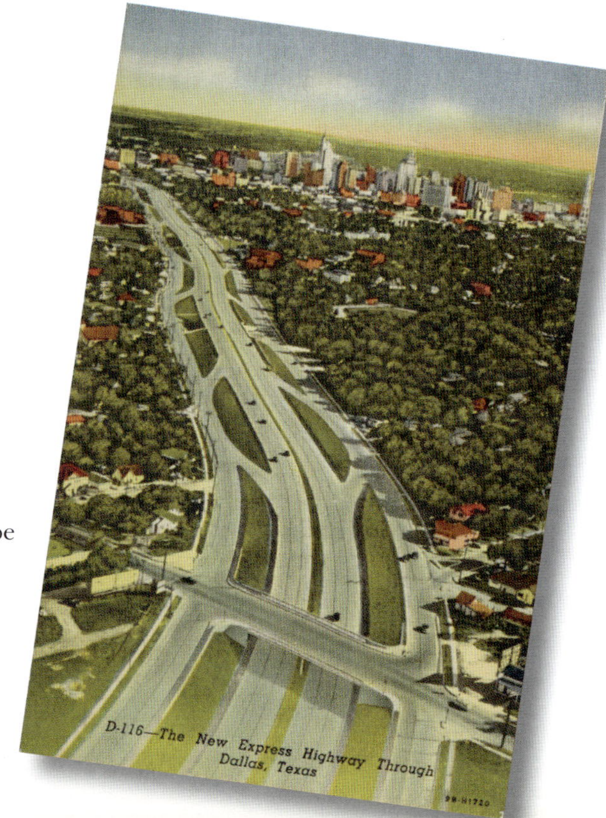

A view of the highway system through Dallas. The city can be seen on the horizon.

Circa 1930s, $2-4

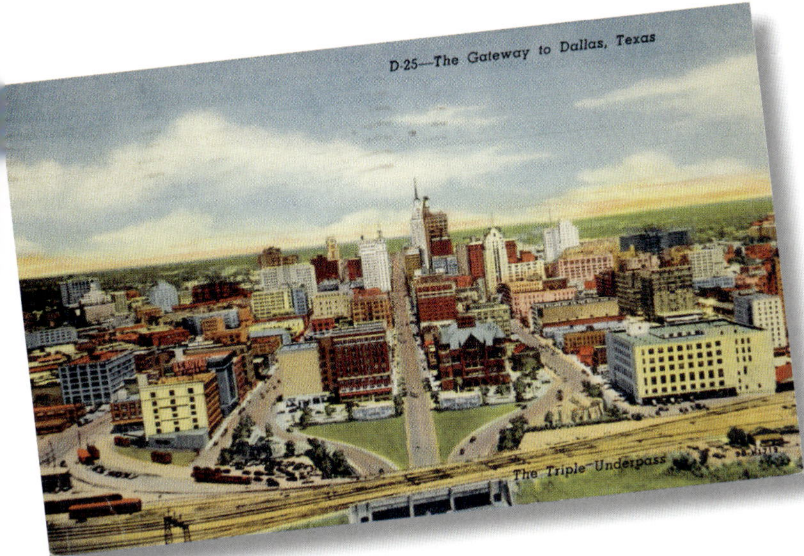

The Triple Underpass of Dallas
was opened in 1936.

Circa 1930s, $2-4 (left)
Circa 1914, $2-4 (below)

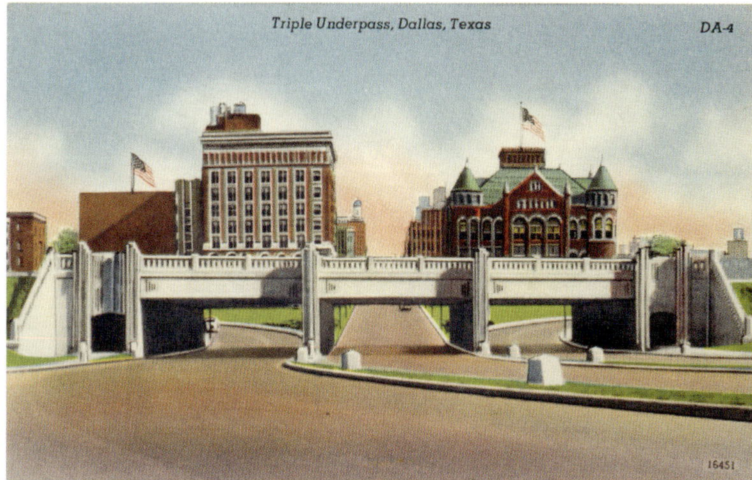

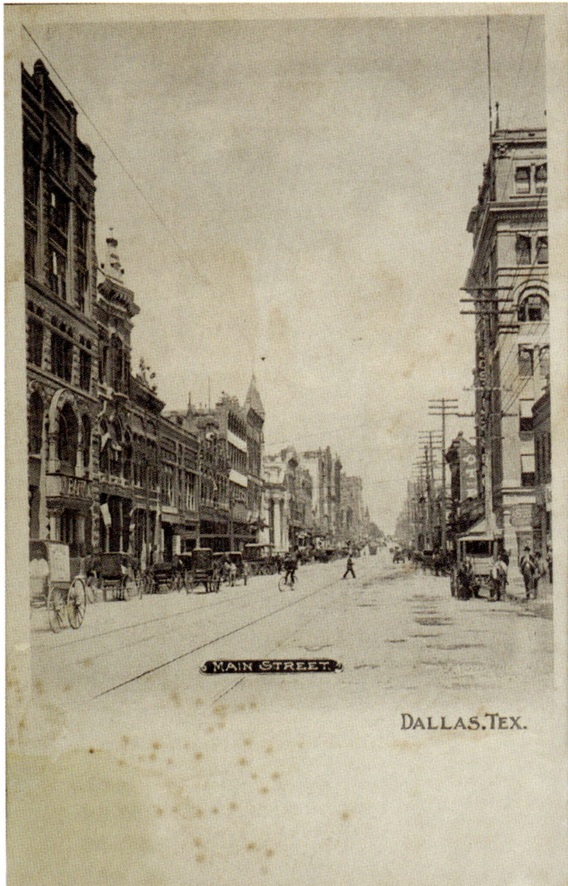

An early view of Main Street.

Circa early 1900s, $14-16

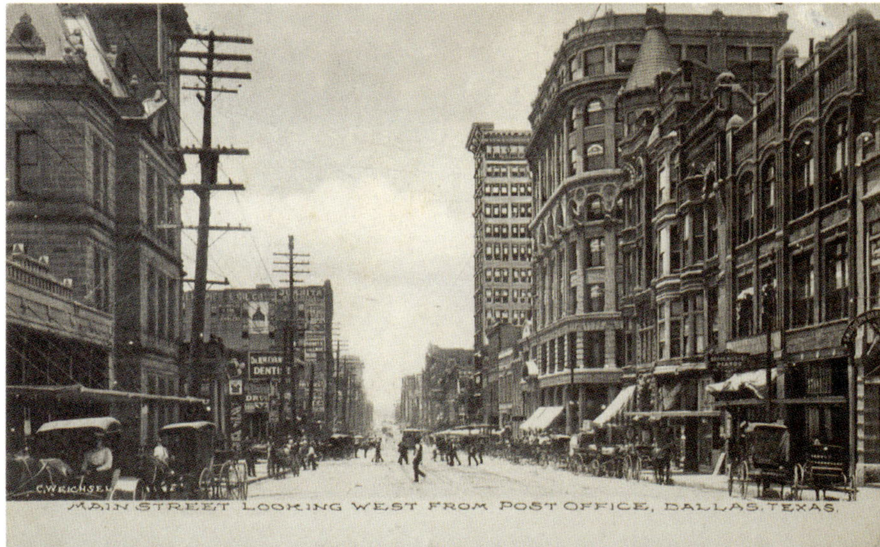

Main Street looking west. You will note the Brooks Mays Piano shop on the right front side of the card. Brook Mays opened a piano dealership in Dallas, with the original store opening in 1901. It became the largest dealership (trading solely in pianos) in the region.

Cancelled 1907, $14-16

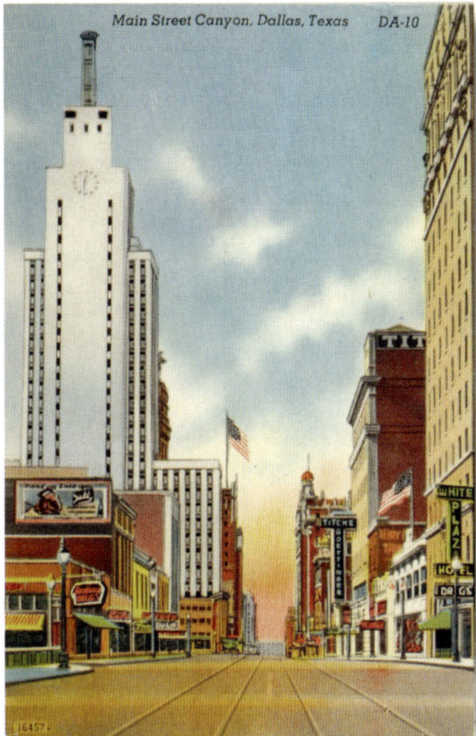

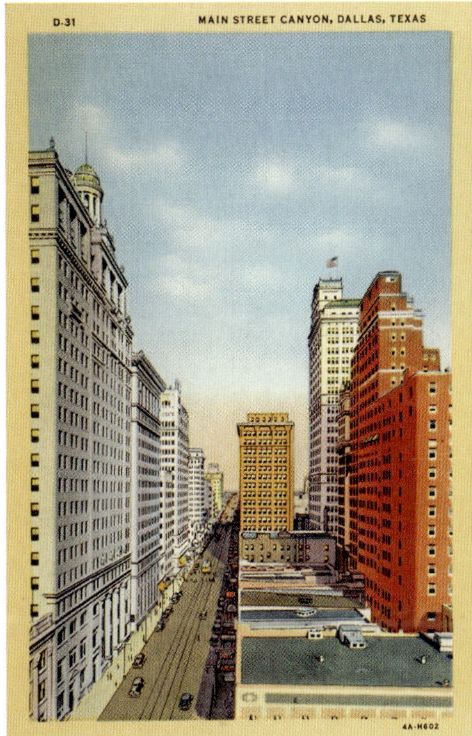

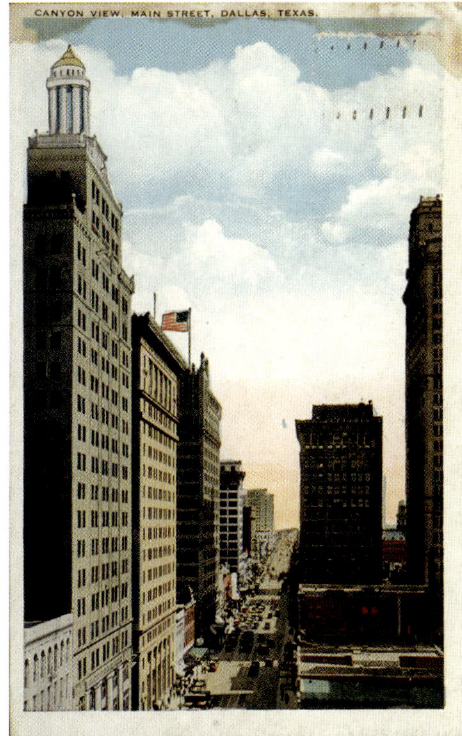

Canyon views of Main Street. Main Street was home to such buildings as the Bush/Kirby Building, the Davis Building, the Interstate Forwarding Building, the Western Union Building, and the Texas Farm and Ranch Building. Titche-Goettinger was part of a very popular department store chain with a store located on Main, its construction beginning in 1928. It was sold, however, during the construction, to Hahn Department Stores.

Circa 1930s, $2-4
Circa 1920s, 2-4
Cancelled 1929, $4-6

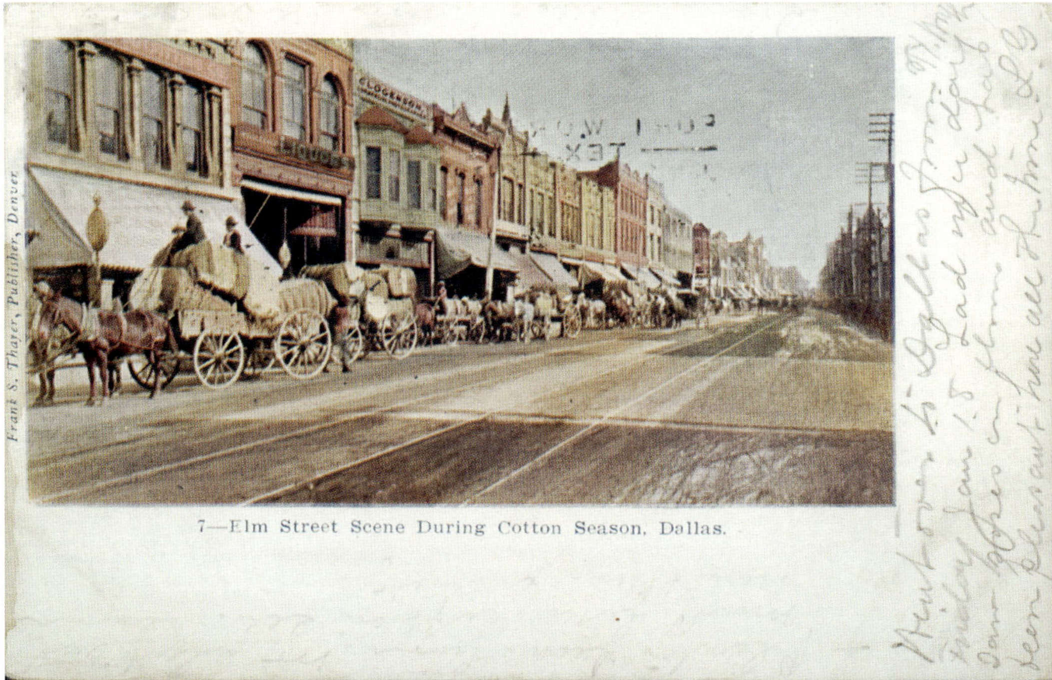

Elm Street during cotton season. The first cotton crop was planted in 1846, and it quickly became a key commodity. Dallas was noted as the nation's largest inland cotton maker.

Cancelled 1907, $6-10

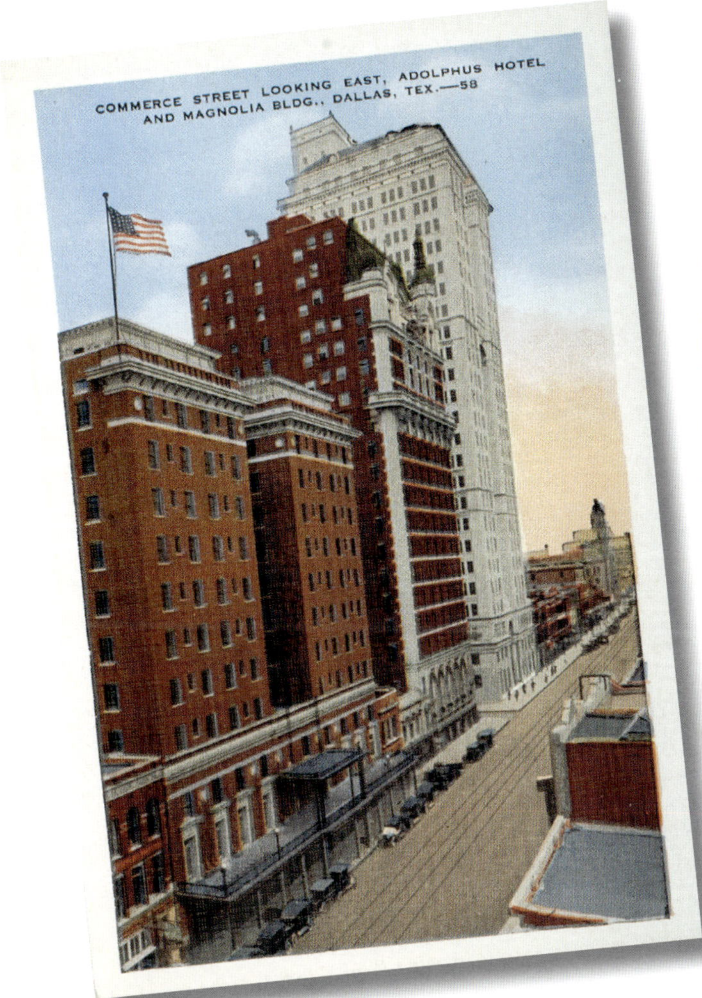

Commerce Street looking eastward gives a glimpse of the Adolphus Hotel and the Magnolia Building. The Magnolia, known later as Socony and Mobile Oil, was built by Magnolia Petroleum. In 1934, a spinning red horse was built on the roof as a symbol of the city.

Circa 1914, $2-4

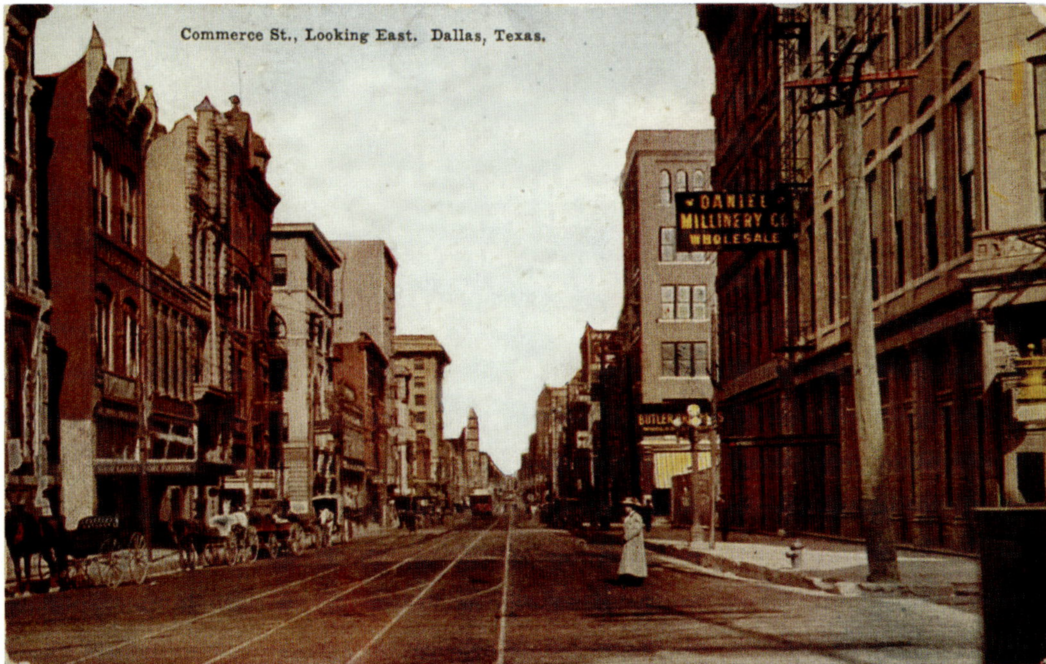

This view of Commerce Street also looks east and shows the Daniel Millinery Co. Wholesale shop. Not only did he found the downtown company, but by 1905, he was a prominent millionaire and business leader of Dallas.

Circa early 1900s, $8-10

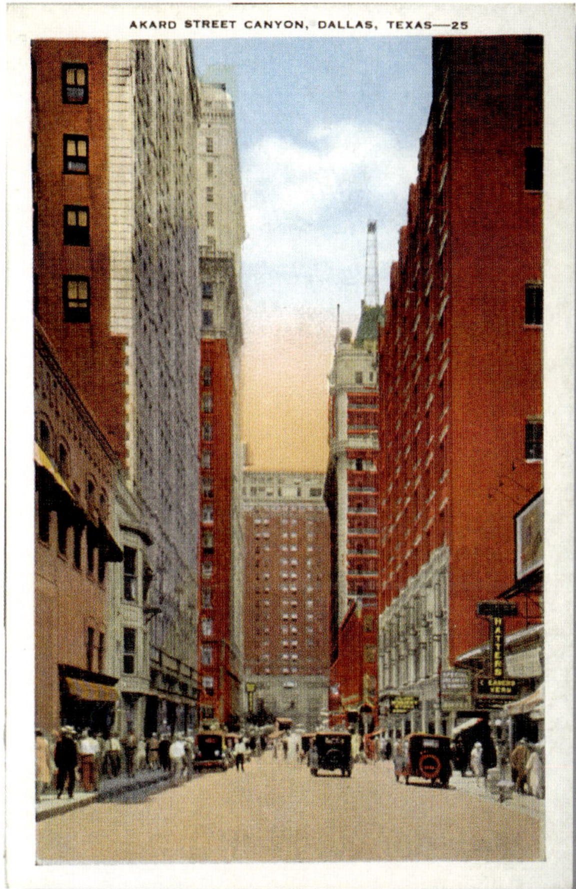

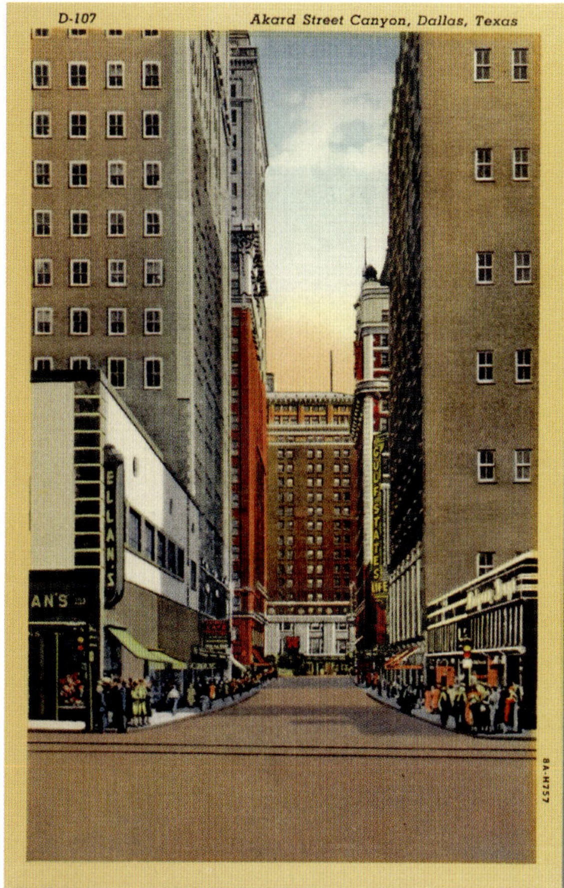

Akard Street Canyon. Akard Street is home to the Federal Reserve Bank, the Magnolia Building (intersecting Commerce), and the Gulf States Life Building. The Gulf States Life Building was constructed in 1927 at the intersections of Akard and Maine along with two other insurance companies nearby. It grew so quickly at this location, that in 1935, seven additional floors were added to the building.

Circa 1920s, $2-4 (left)
Circa 1914, $2-4 (right)

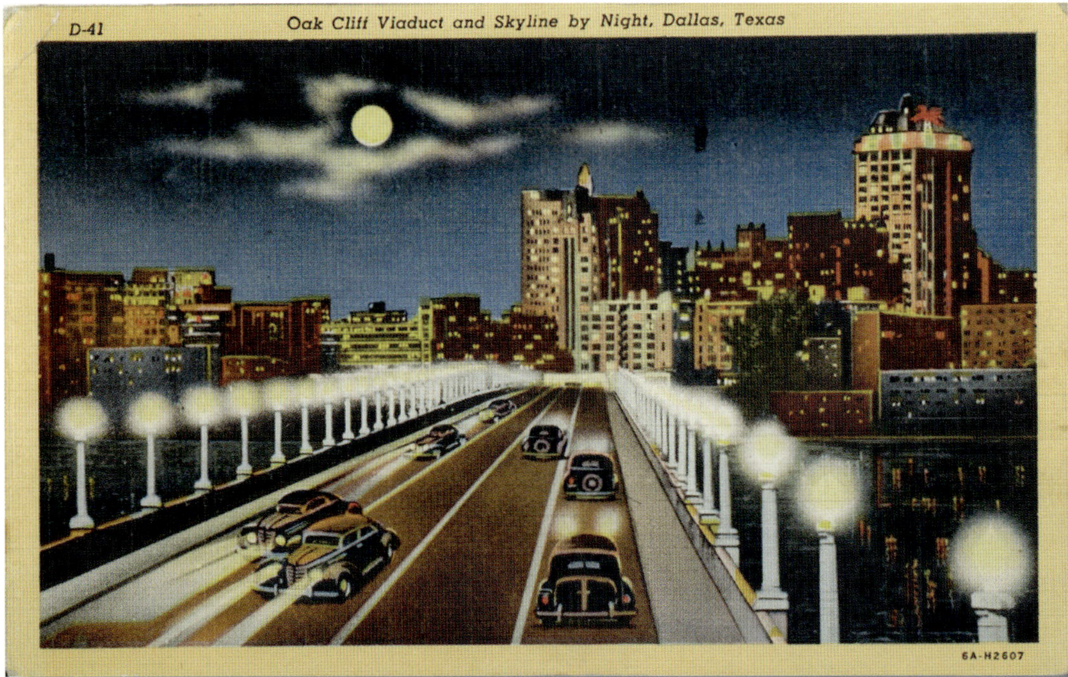

The Dallas-Oak Cliff Viaduct at night. You can see the red flying horse maintained atop the Magnolia Building from the bridge. Interestingly, Clyde Barrow (of Bonnie and Clyde fame) camped beneath this at the age of thirteen.

Circa 1930s, $2-4

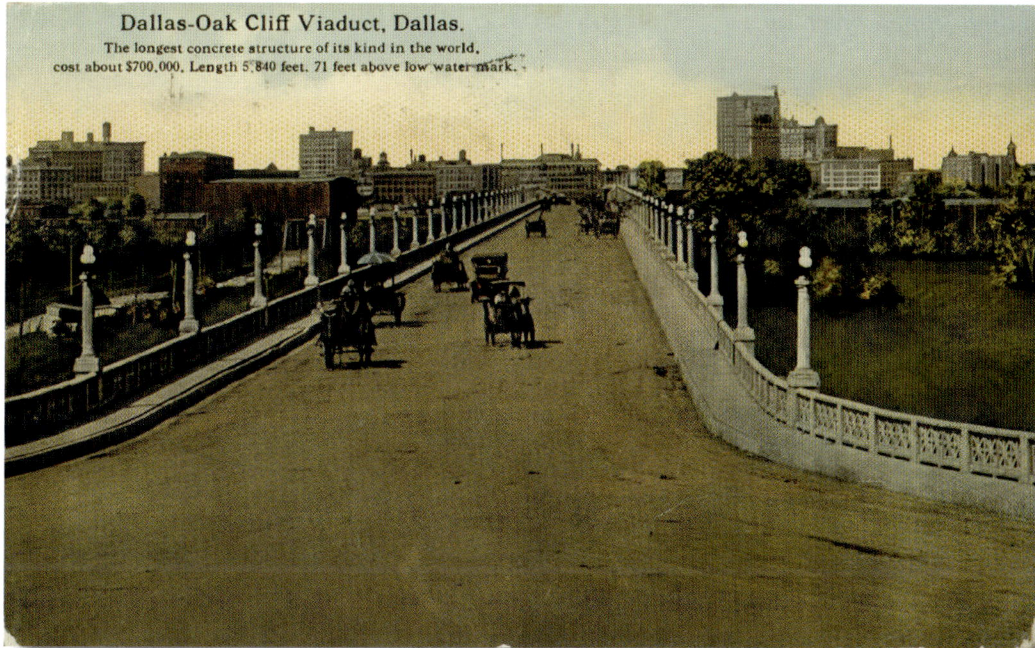

The planning phase for the building of the Dallas-Oak Cliff Viaduct began after a horrendous flood dealt a financial and societal blow in 1908. In 1926, work began in an attempt to create levees that would redirect the river and move the banks away from the downtown area.

Circa Early 1900s, $6-8

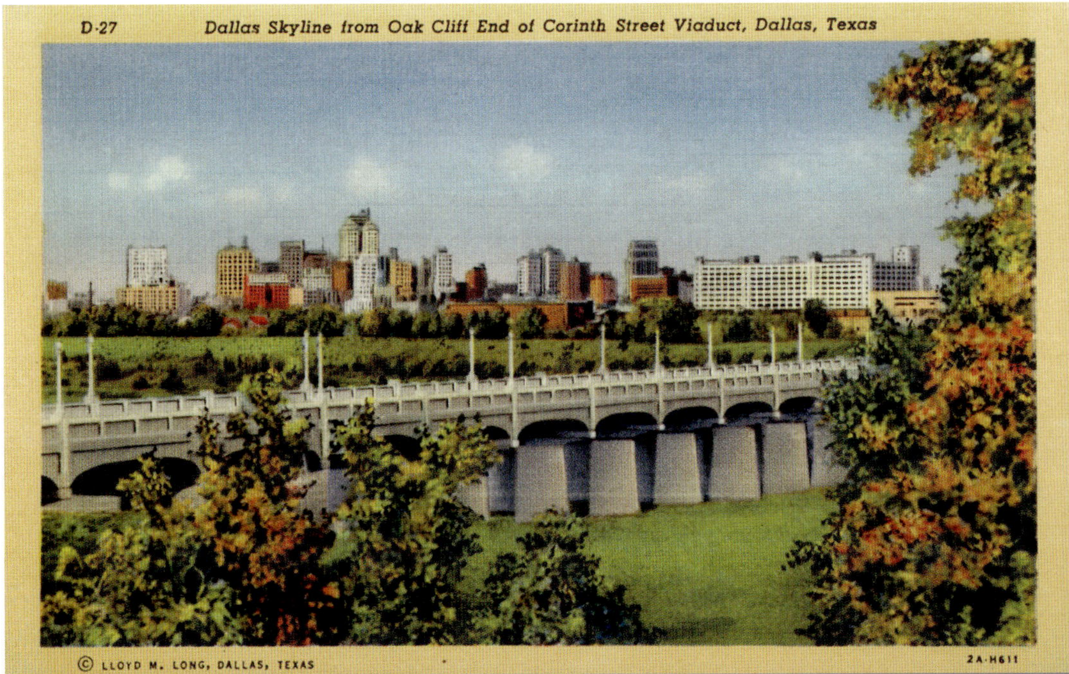

A picturesque view of the viaduct and skyline of Dallas. Now called the Houston Street Viaduct, it is still in use.

Circa 1914, $2-4

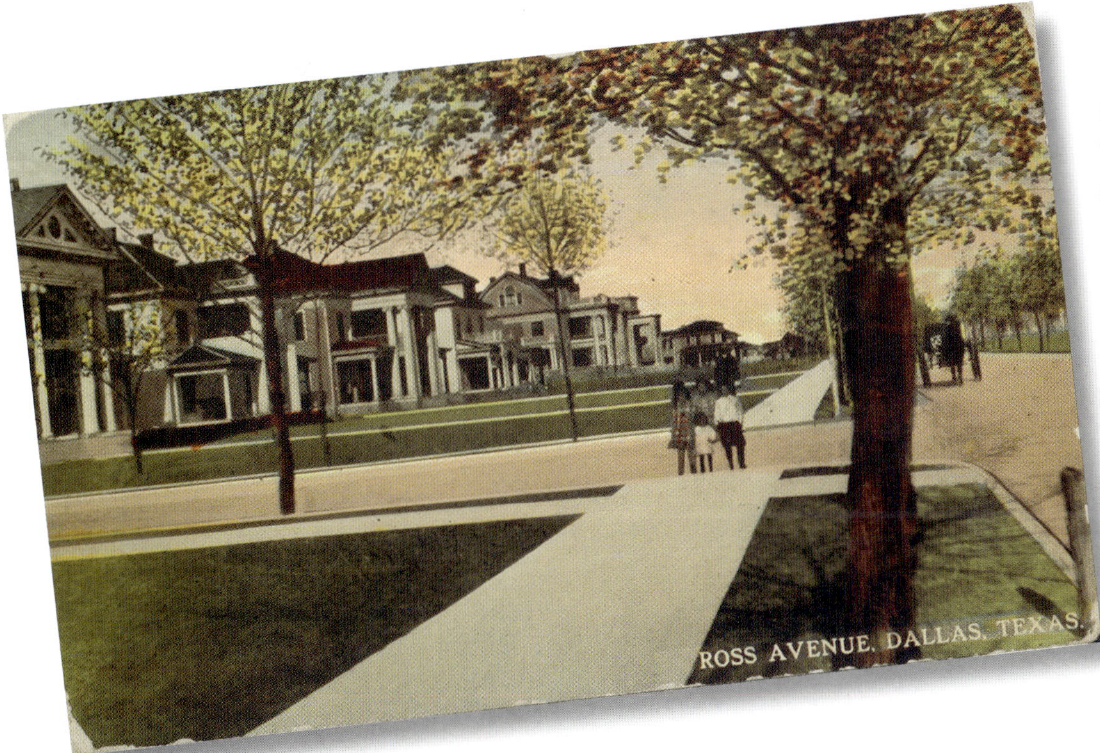

Ross Avenue, a scenic depiction of residential pride.

Circa 1910, $4-6

Scenic Dallas

Though Dallas has been an important part of America's overall economics, one cannot forget the unbridled beauty and serenity of her land. Vibrant colors, grassy trails and landscapes, and cityscapes alive with culture await you in Dallas.

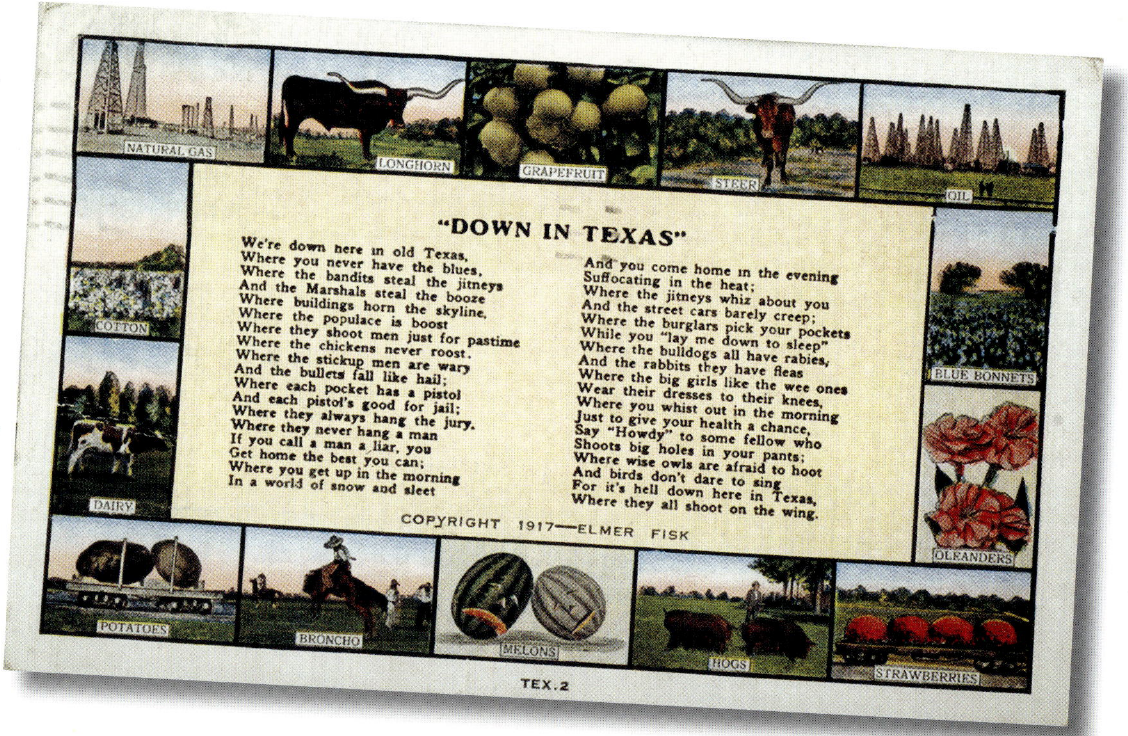

Cancelled 1940, $2-4

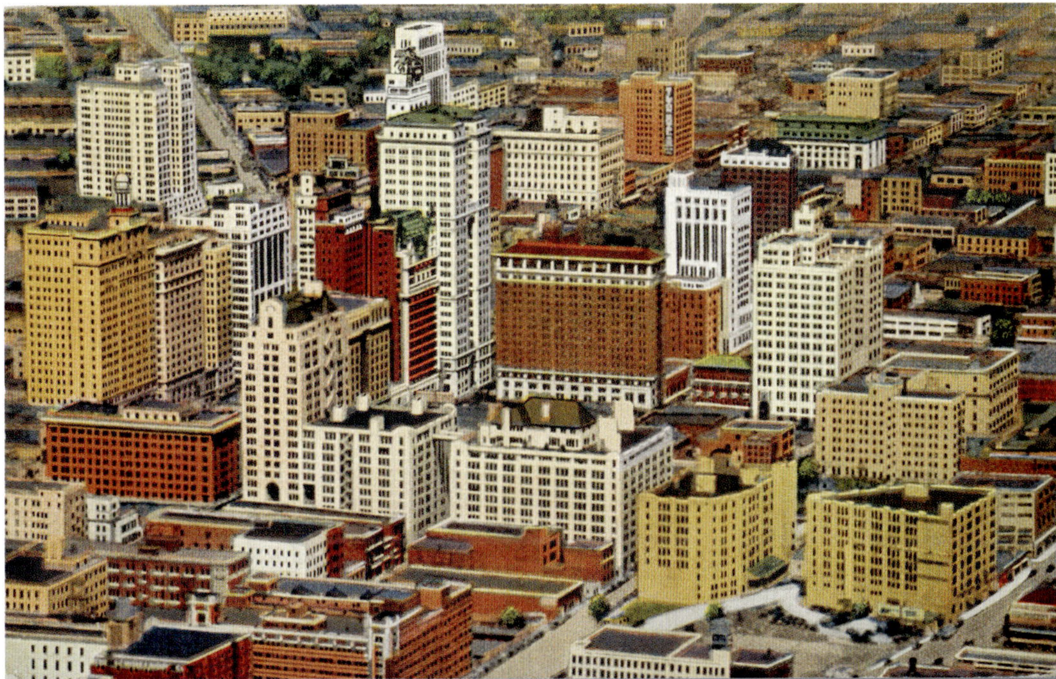

The downtown metropolis of Dallas.

Cancelled 1944, $4-6

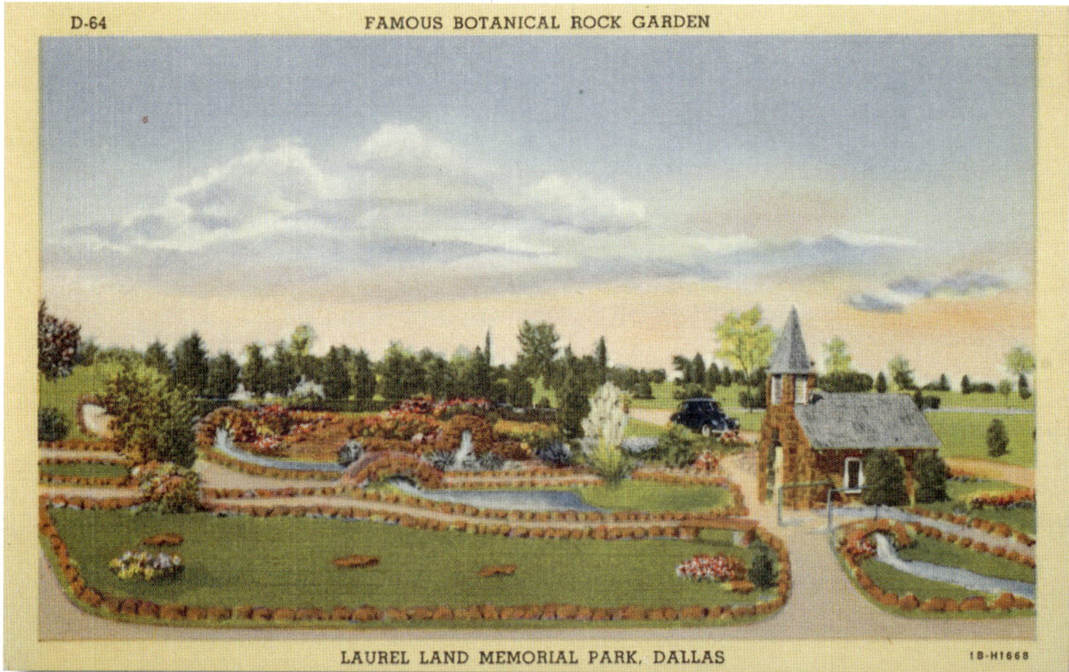

Laurel Land Memorial Park at the Botanical Rock Garden. J. D. Tippit is buried at this park. Tippit was the man who was gunned down by Lee Harvey Oswald on the Oak Cliff side-street just after the assassination of President John F. Kennedy. Tippit was declared a hero for trying to stop Oswald's escape.

Circa 1914, $2-4

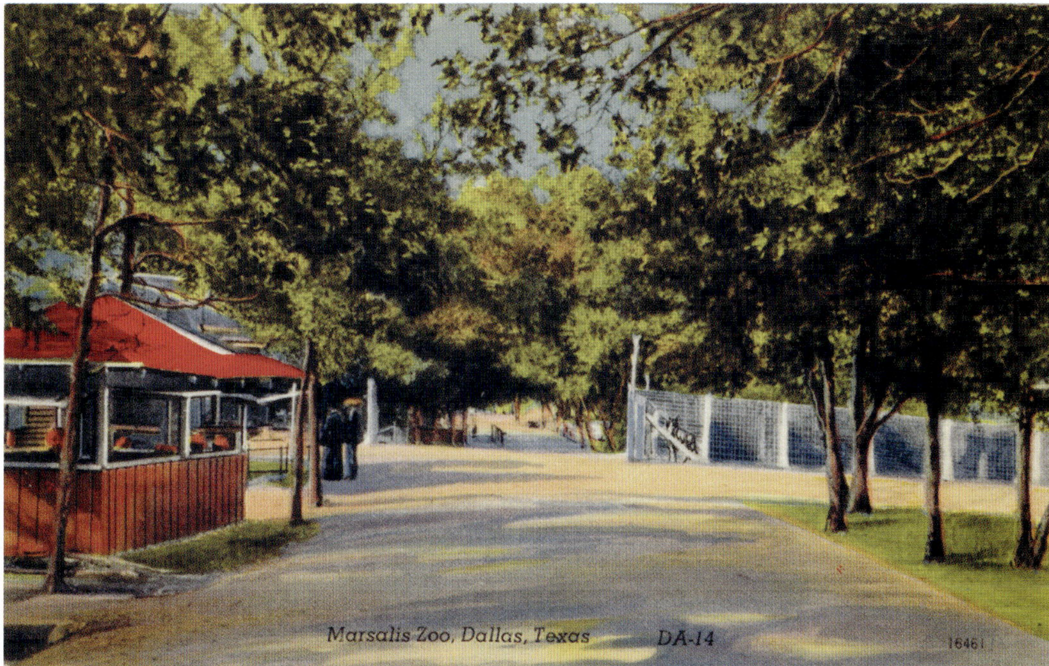

The Marsalis Zoo in Dallas. Now called the Dallas Zoo, this municipal zoological garden was founded in 1888.

Circa 1914, $2-4

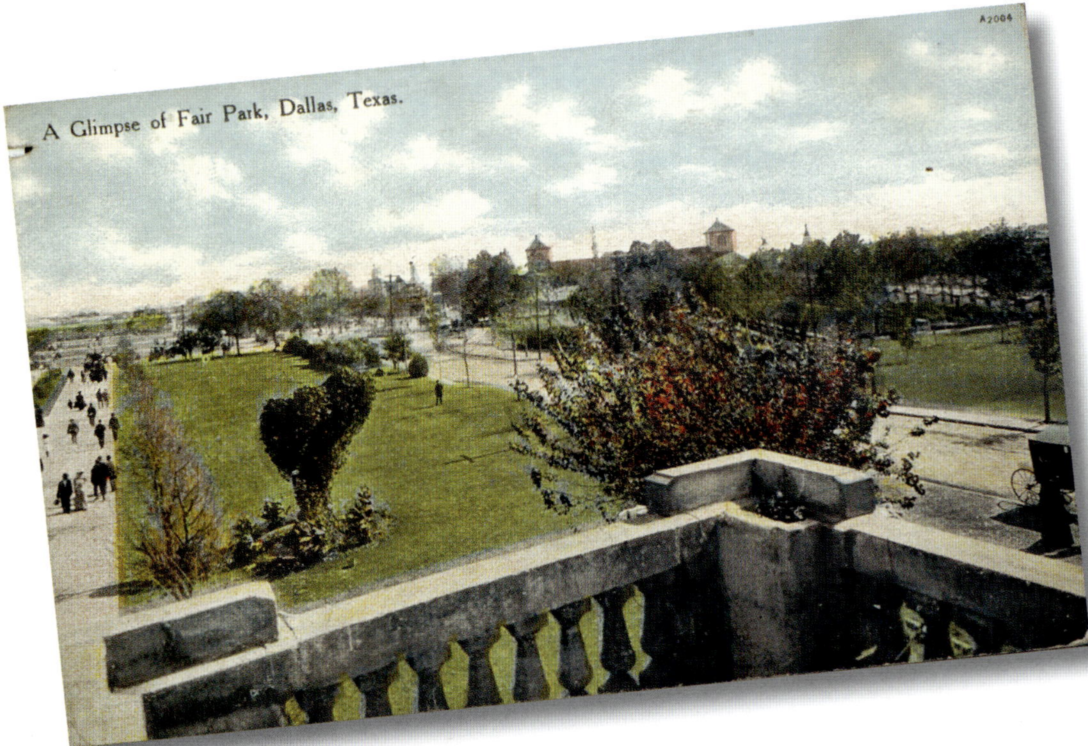

A leisurely stroll on a lovely day along the paths of Fair Park.

Circa 1914, $2-4

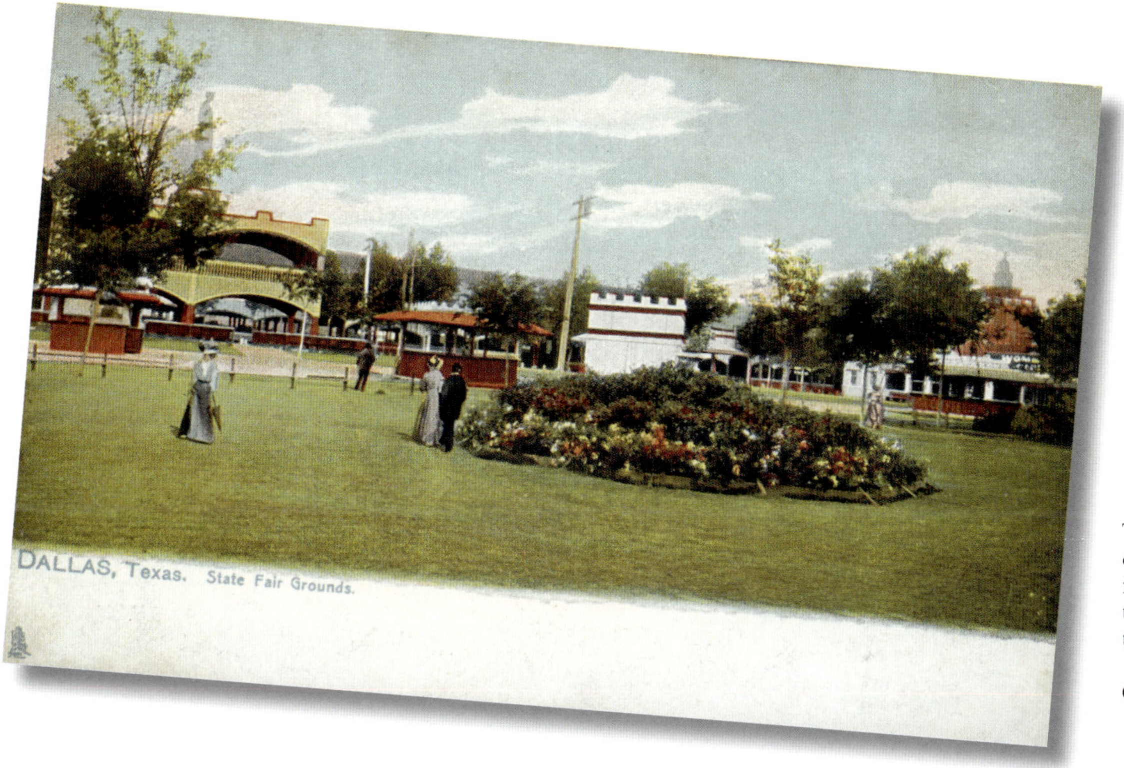

The State Fair grounds, covering eight acres, was a draw for tourism in Texas, bringing hundreds of thousands of visitors to Dallas in the early 1900s.

Circa 1914, $4-6

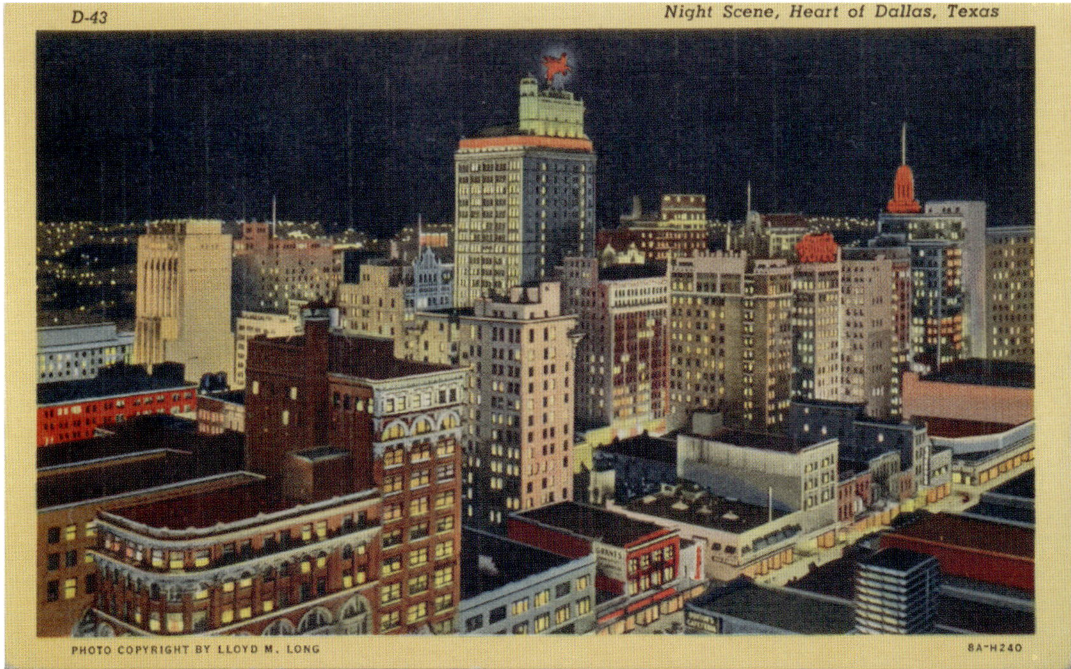

A night scene showing the heart of downtown. The flying red horse of the Magnolia Building is like a beacon in the night.

Circa 1914, $2-4

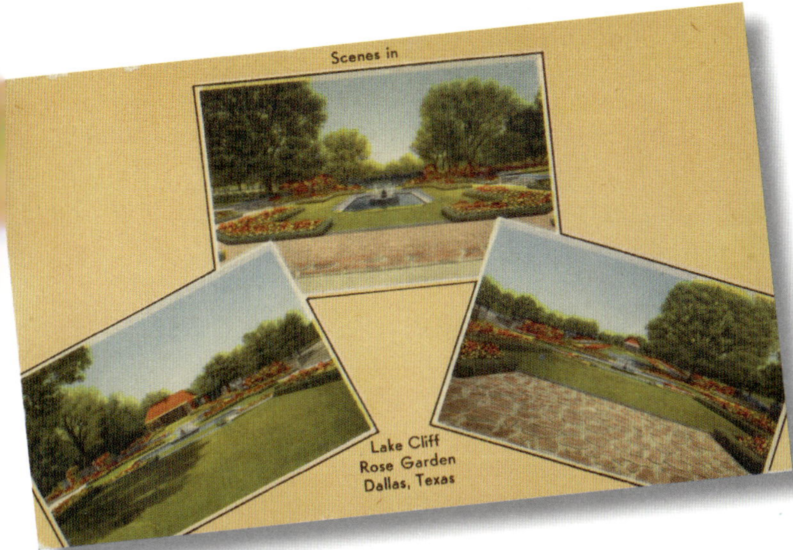

The Lake Cliff Rose Garden. Dallas is known for its lovely garden park landscapes, and this garden is noted as one of the most beautiful, with thousands of blooming roses.

Circa 1914, $2-4

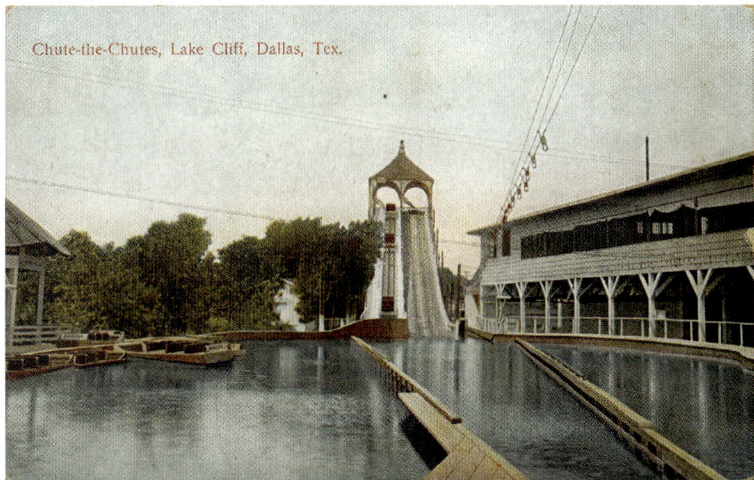

Originally called Lake Llewellyn, Lake Cliff is a freshwater body in the northern part of the Oak Cliff area of Dallas.

Circa 1914, $8-10

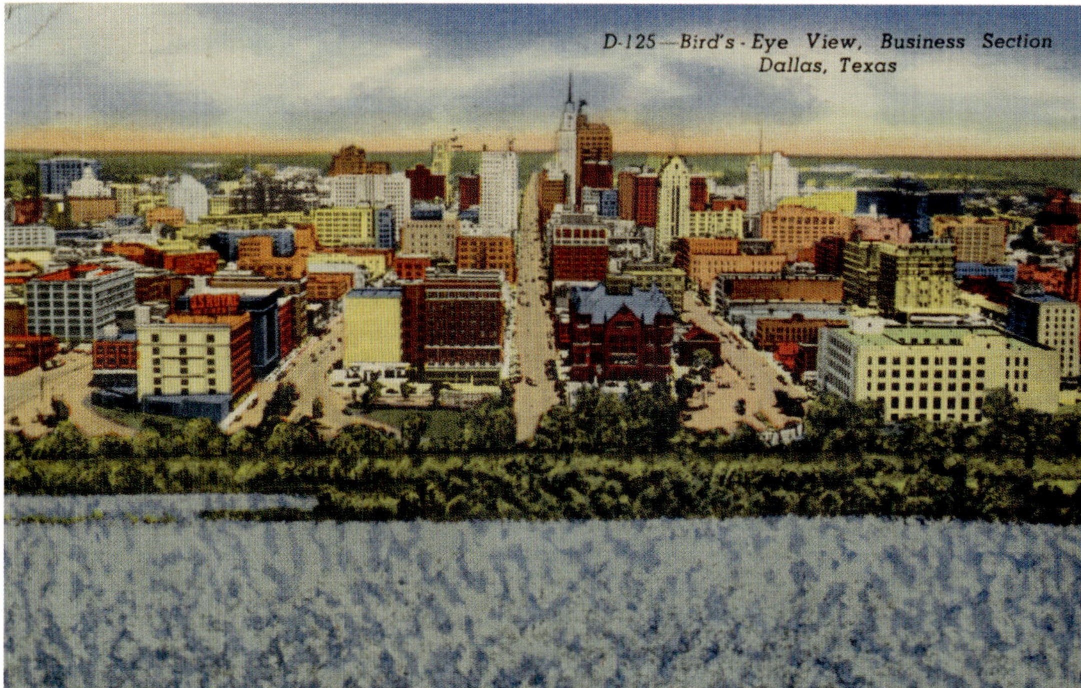

An aerial view of the downtown business section of Dallas.

Cancelled 1952, $2-4

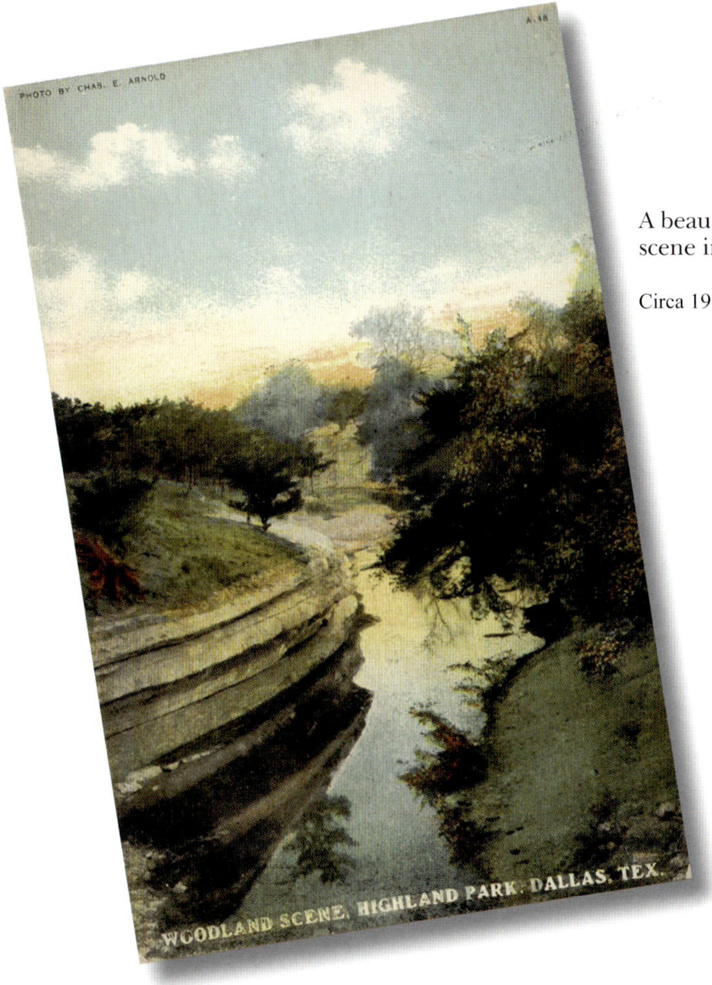

A beautiful woodland scene in Highland Park.

Circa 1914, $2-4

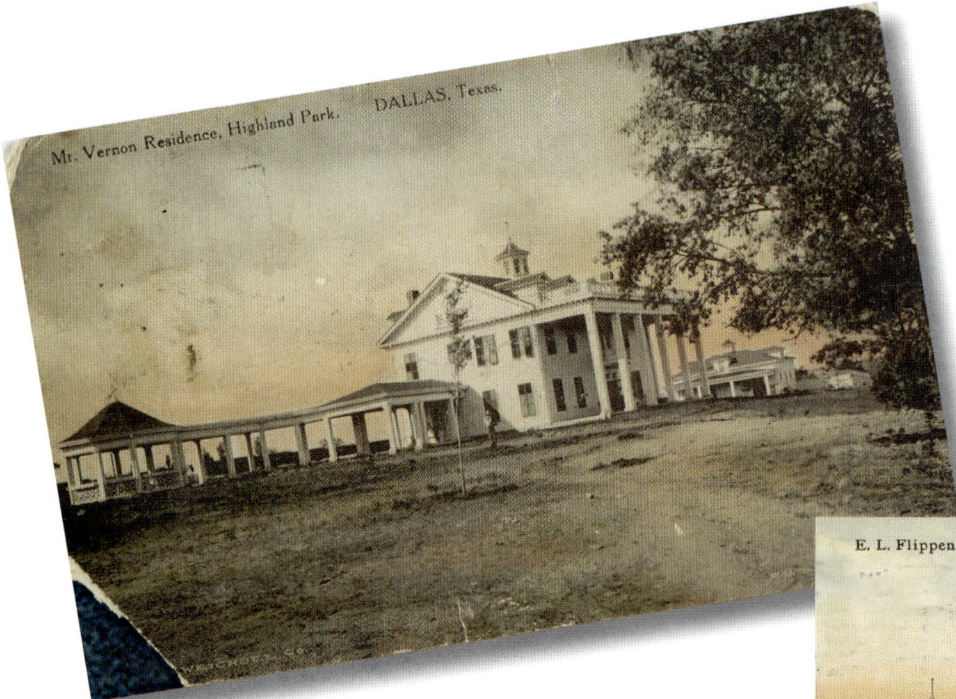

The Mt. Vernon Residence in Highland Park. Highland Park is an area in the central part of Dallas County very near to Dallas. A second view of the same residence is recorded as belonging to E. L. Flippen.

Circa 1914, $6-8 (left)
Cancelled 1911, $6-8 (below)

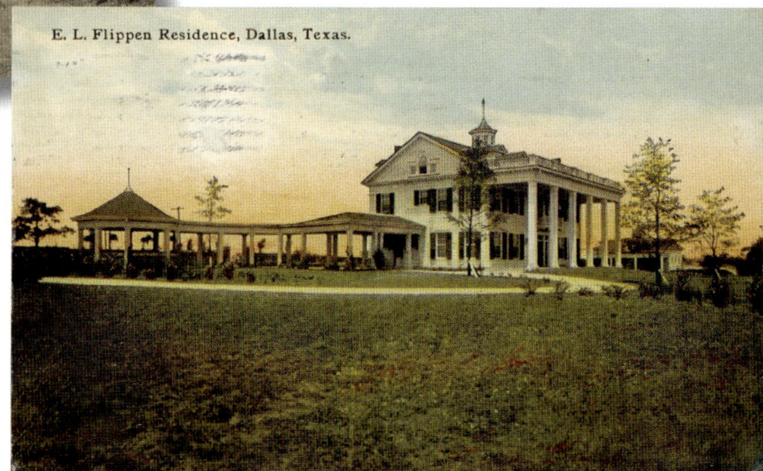

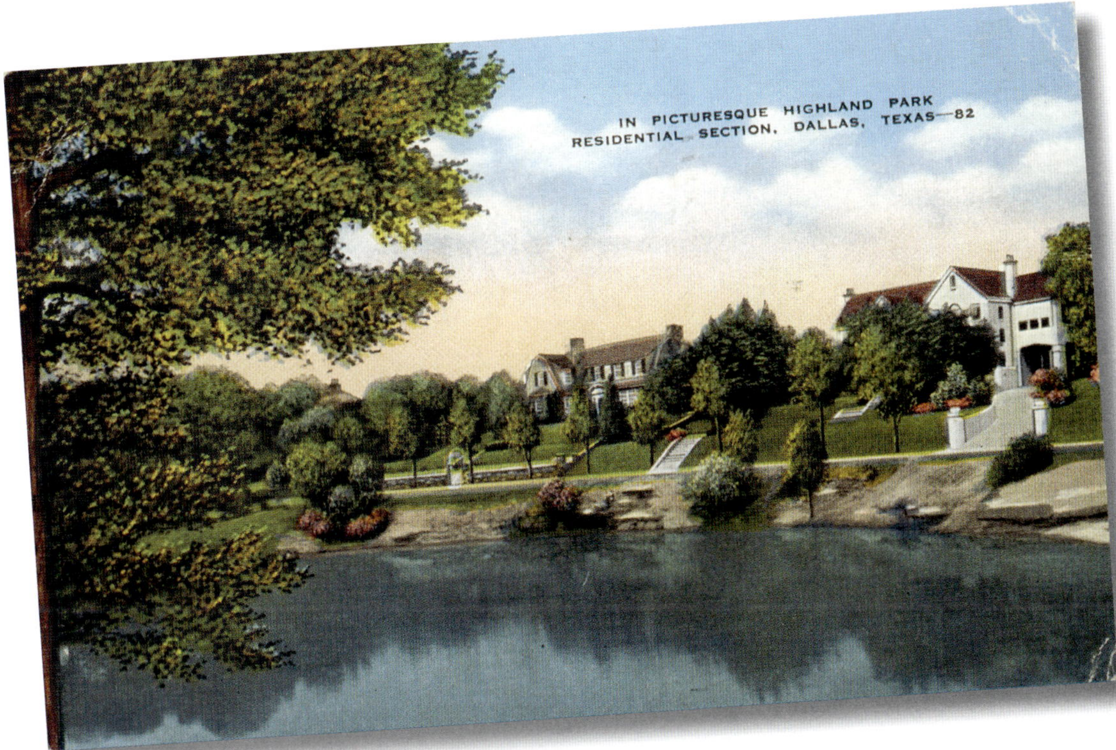

Because of its proximity to Dallas, Highland Park's population, by the early 1930s, grew to approximately 8,400, and even included a few businesses.

Cancelled 1942, $2-4

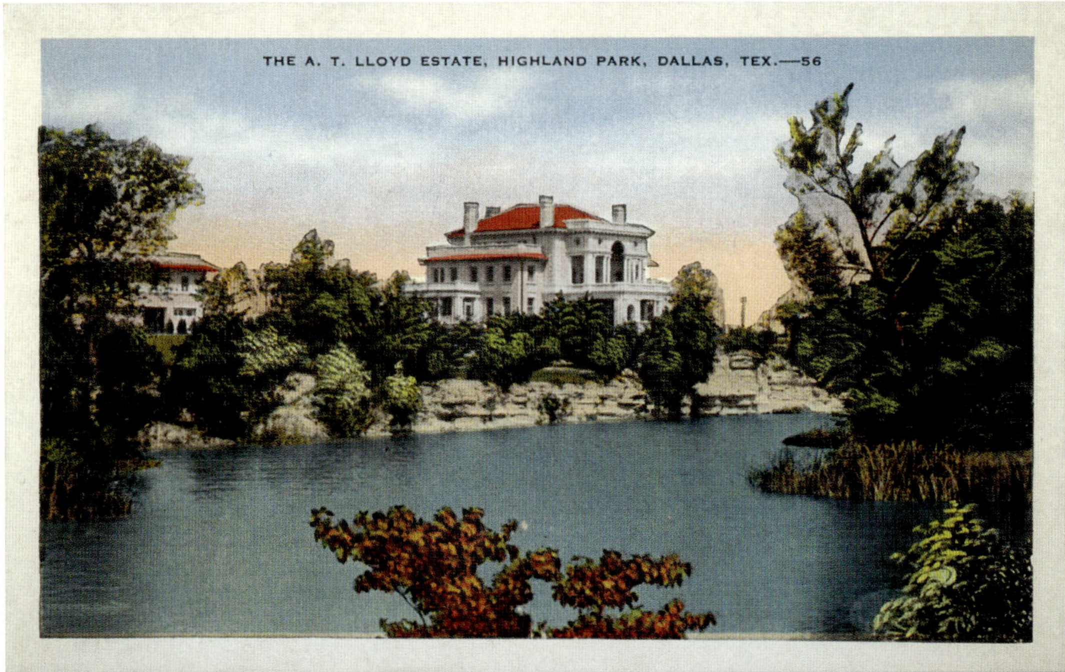

Another scenic view of the residences in Highland Park.

Circa 1914, $2-4

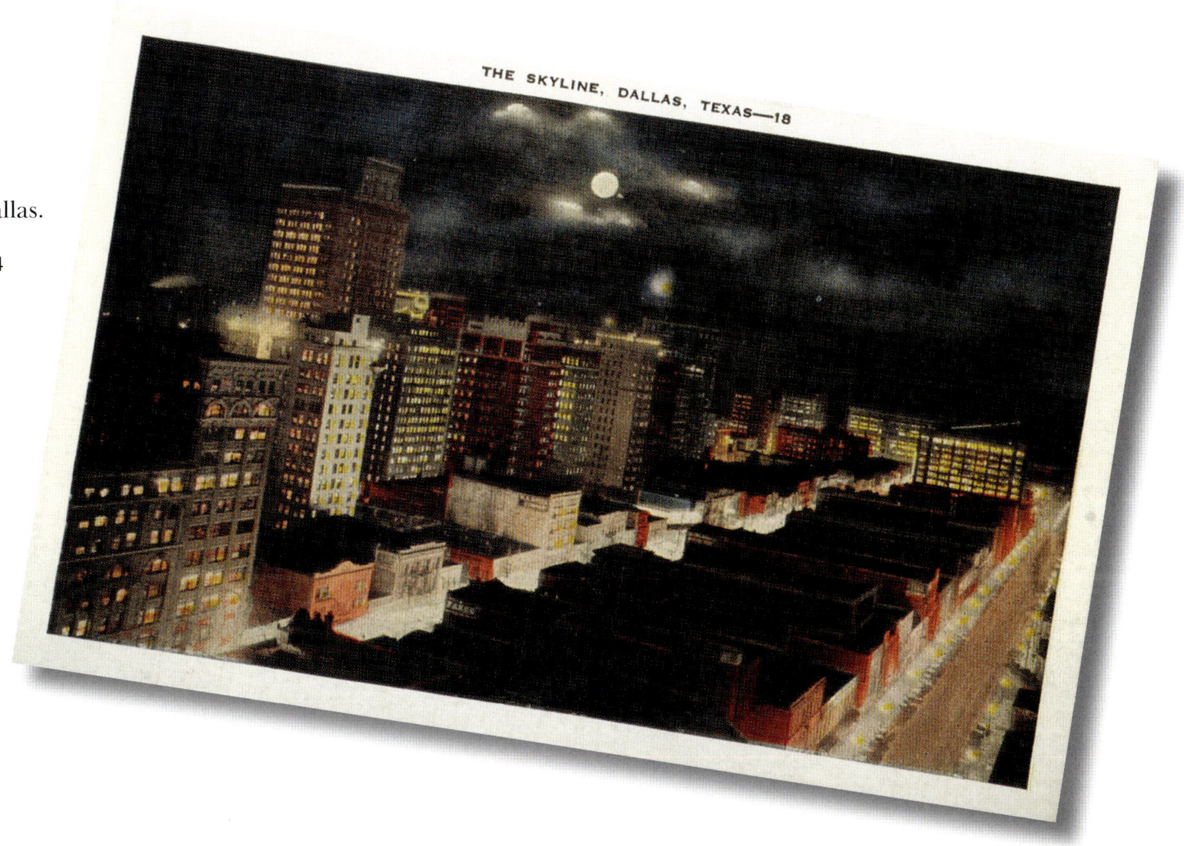

A night in Dallas.

Circa 1914, $2-4

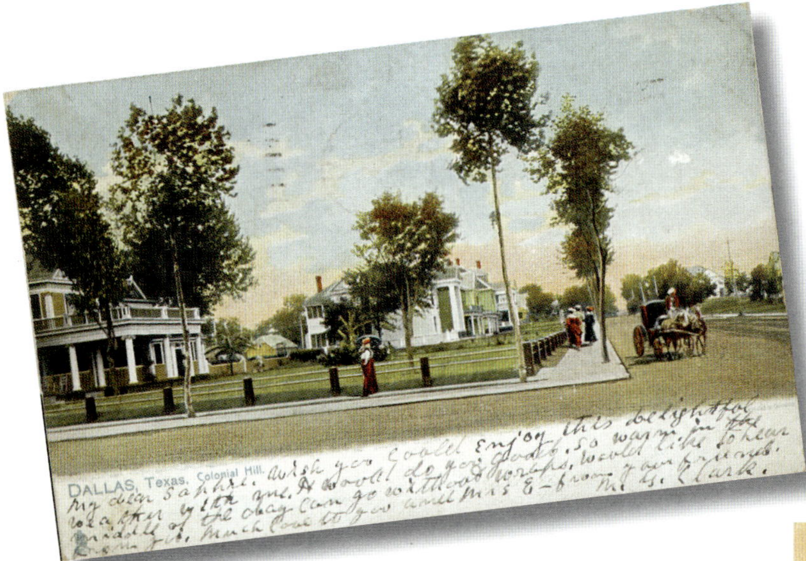

Colonial Hill is a suburb of Dallas making it a lovely, high-class residential community for those needing to be near the city. The area is known for its extensive and well-kept grounds.

Cancelled 1907, $6-8

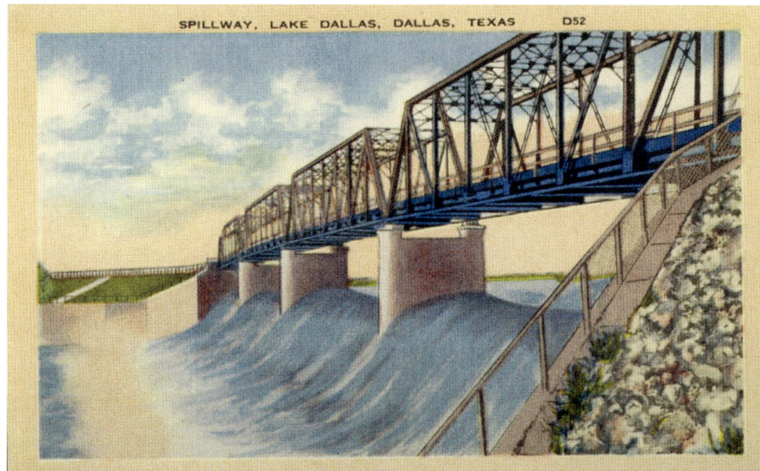

A resort community on the shores of Lewisville Lake, Lake Dallas is located between Dallas and Denton, Texas. The view here is of the spillway.

Circa 1914, $2-4

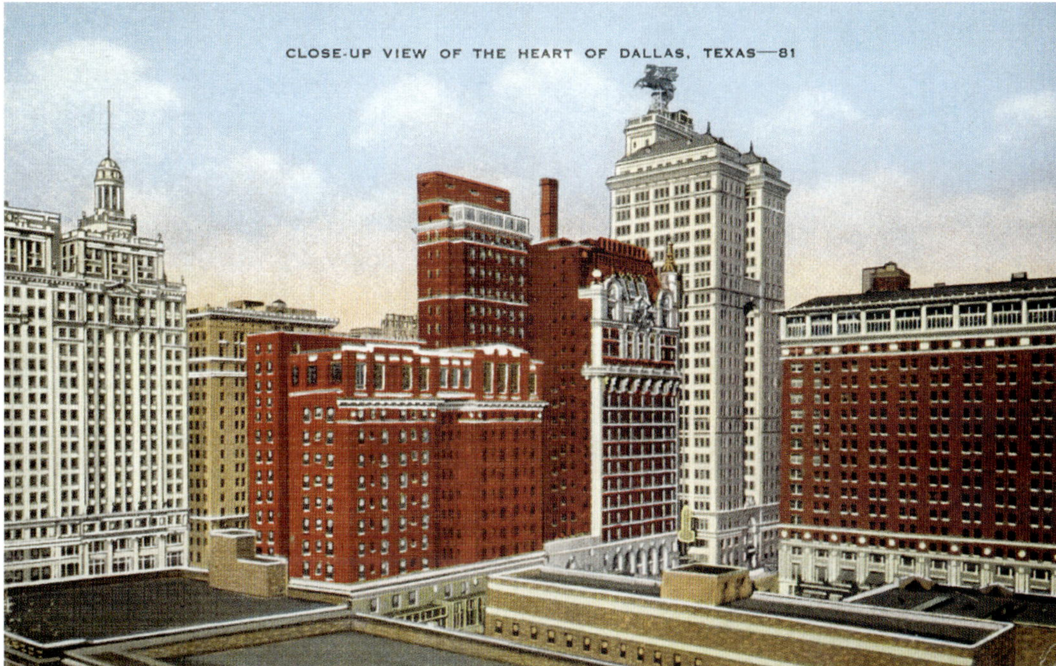

A daylight view of downtown Dallas still shows how prominent the symbol of Texas is—the flying horse on the Magnolia Building stands high among all the high-rise buildings.

Circa 1910, $4-6

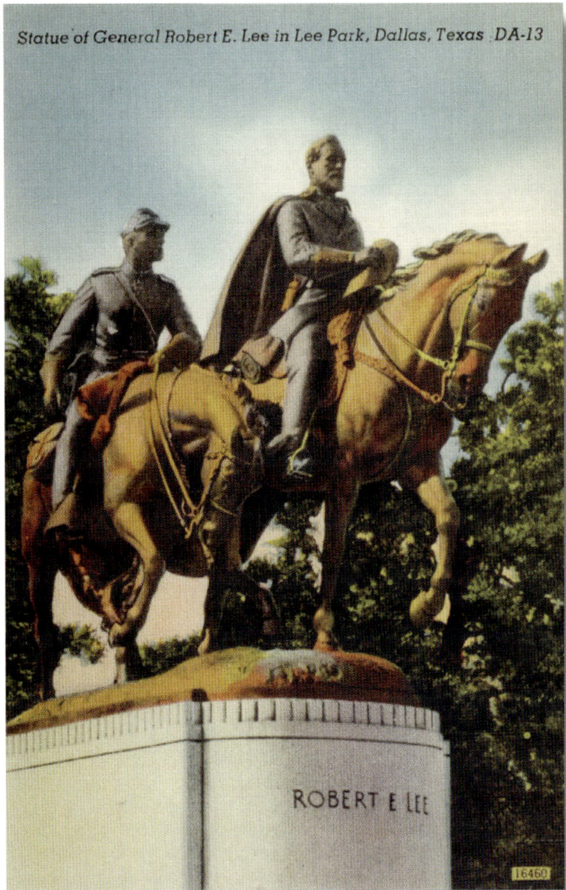

Robert E. Lee statue in Lee Park. The park, originally called Oak Lawn Park, was built in 1903. The statue was unveiled in 1936 in honor of General Lee.

Circa 1930s, $2-4

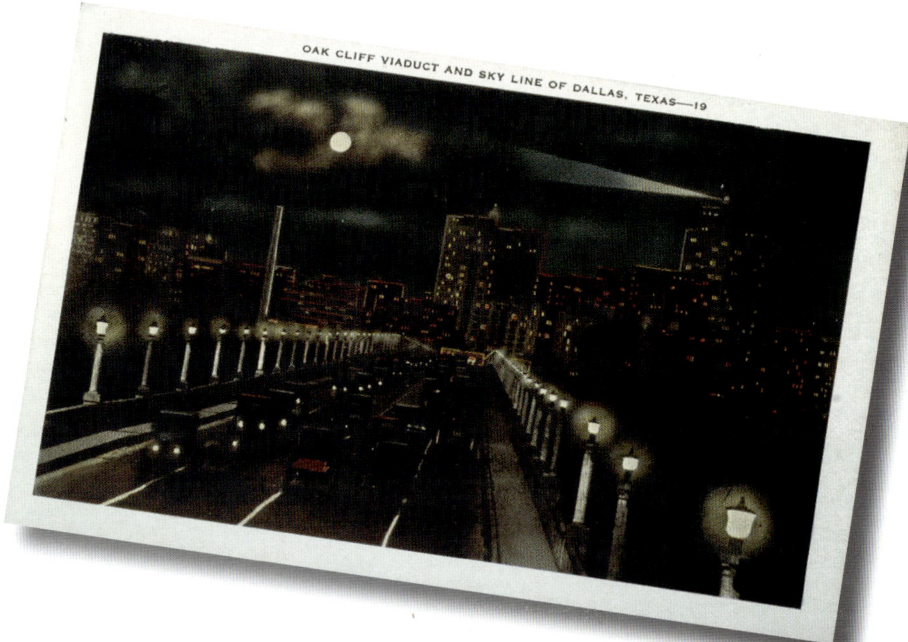

The Oak Cliff Viaduct lit up by the lanterns on the bridge. The viaduct was designed and built at the very beginning of the automobile age according to historical preservation experts.

Circa 1920s, $2-4

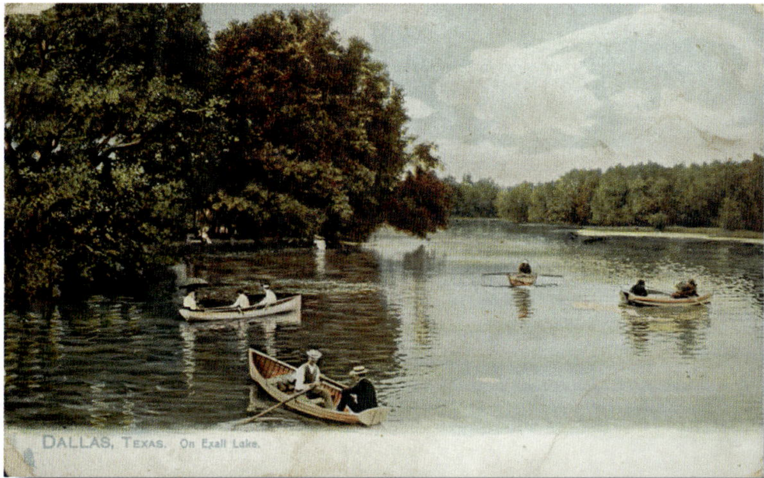

Exall Lake. Henry Exall was a Dallas leader in development, and built one of the city's first skyscrapers, as well as being an important part of the expansion of Highland Park. He constructed a dam on Turtle Creek, in 1890, to make the Exall Lake. The lake became a popular resort area.

Cancelled 1909, $4-6

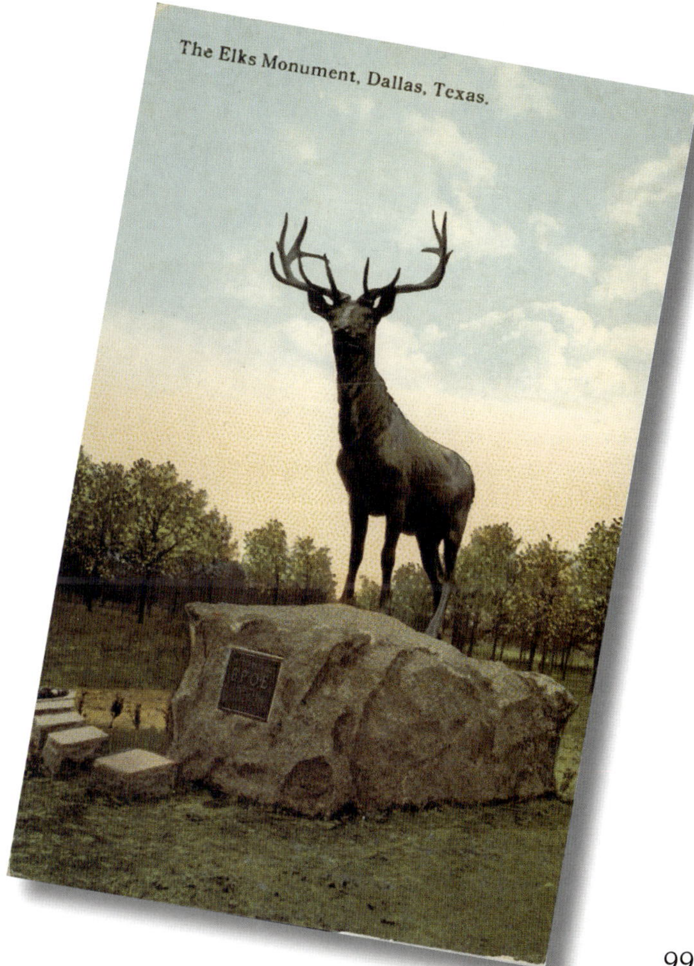

The Elks Monument. The Benevolent and Protective Order of the Elks, Lodge #71, is the oldest lodge in the state and the only one in the city of Dallas. It was founded in 1888.

Circa 1910, $2-4

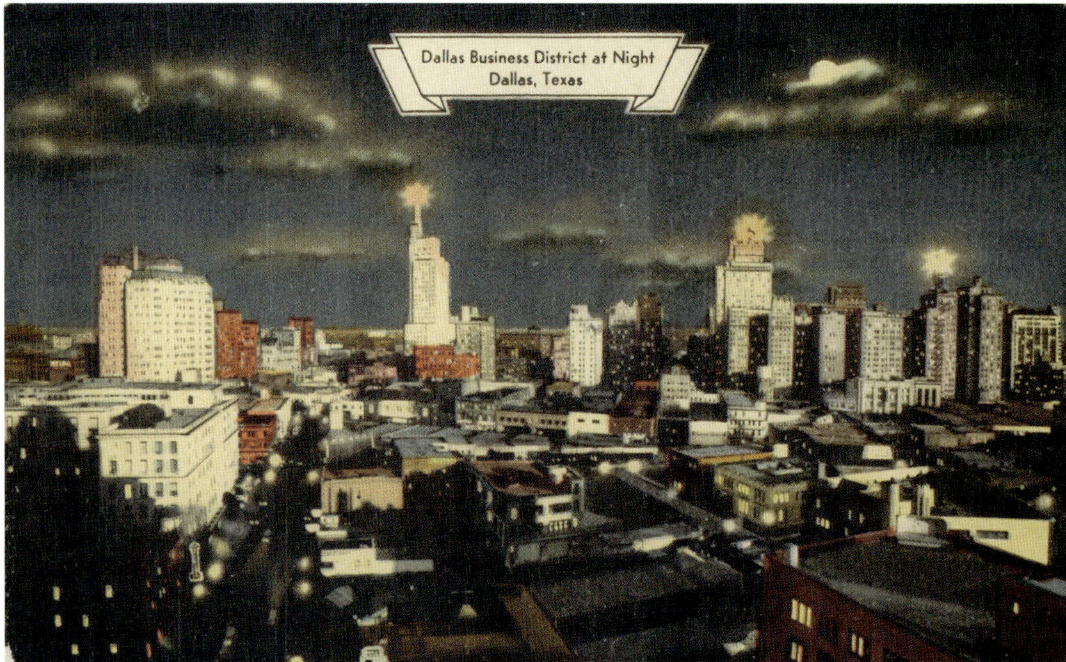

A view of the downtown skyline at night.

Circa 1930s, $2-4

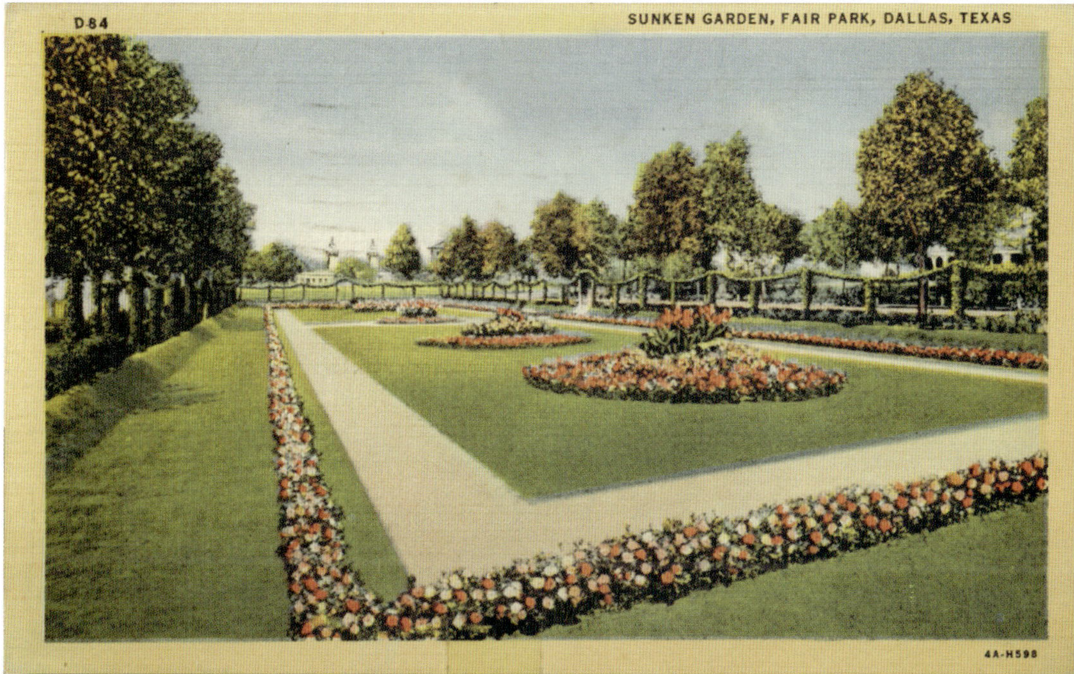

The Sunken Garden as shown at the Arboretum in the Botanical Gardens in Fair Park.

Cancelled 1948, $1914, $2-4

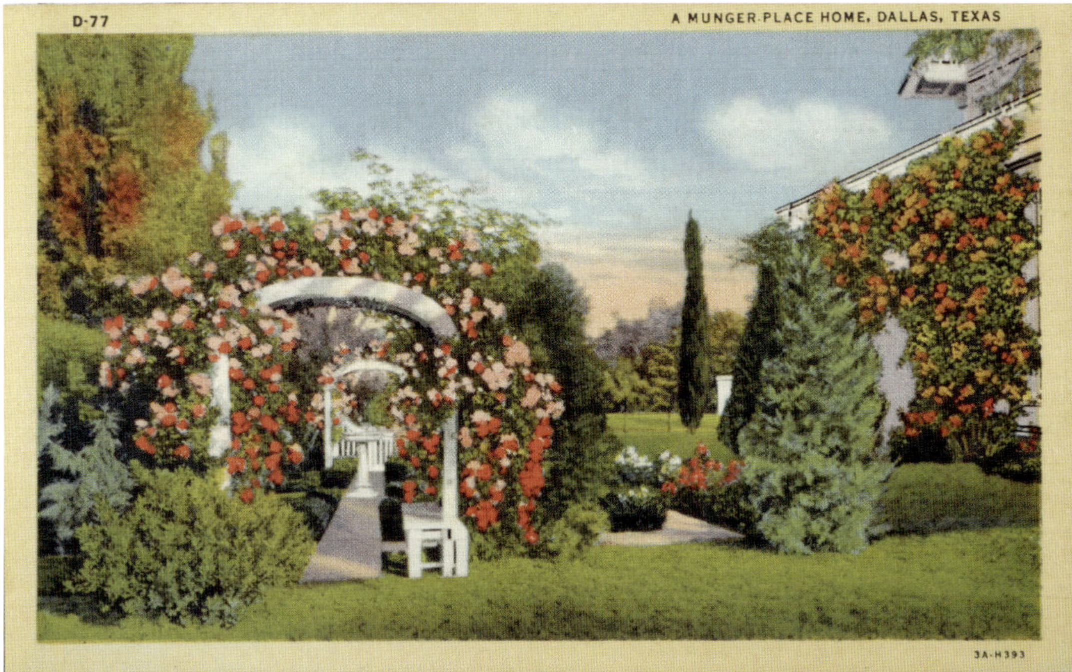

A Munger Place Home. Robert S. Munger and his brother, Collett, carefully planned a community to attract well-to-do city folk to their deed-restricted neighborhood. Close to Dallas, homes here had to be at least two stories high, cost at least $2,000 (a sizeable amount in those days), and no house could face a side street. Catering to leading businessmen, the neighborhood infrastructure included sidewalks, paved roads, trees, and electric lighting.

Circa 1914, $2-4

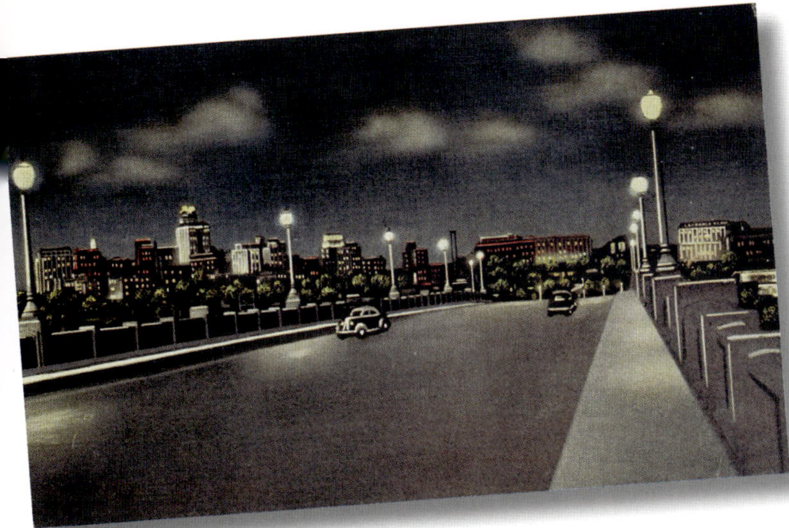

Another view of the famous viaduct roadway.

Circa 1930s, $2-4

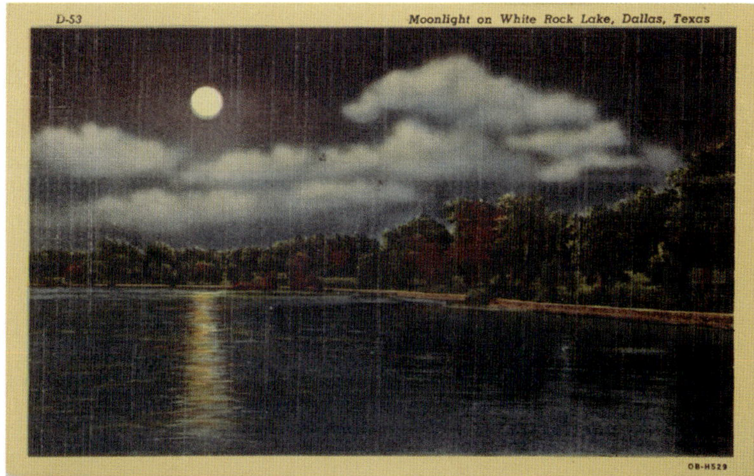

The White Rock Lake was formerly a water supply reservoir for the city of Dallas. In 1929, the area was released by the Water Board to the City Park Department for purposes of leisure.

Circa 1914, $2-4

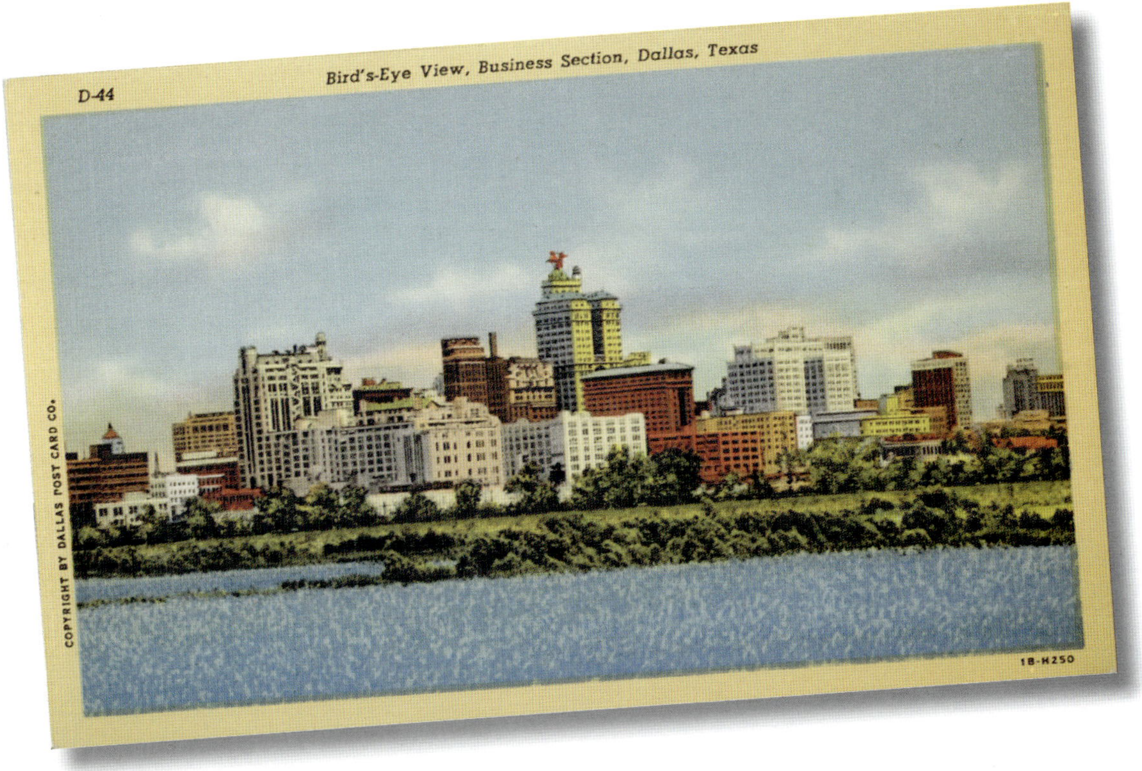

A bird's-eye view of Dallas showing the high-rise buildings and scenic skyline.

Circa 1914, $2-4

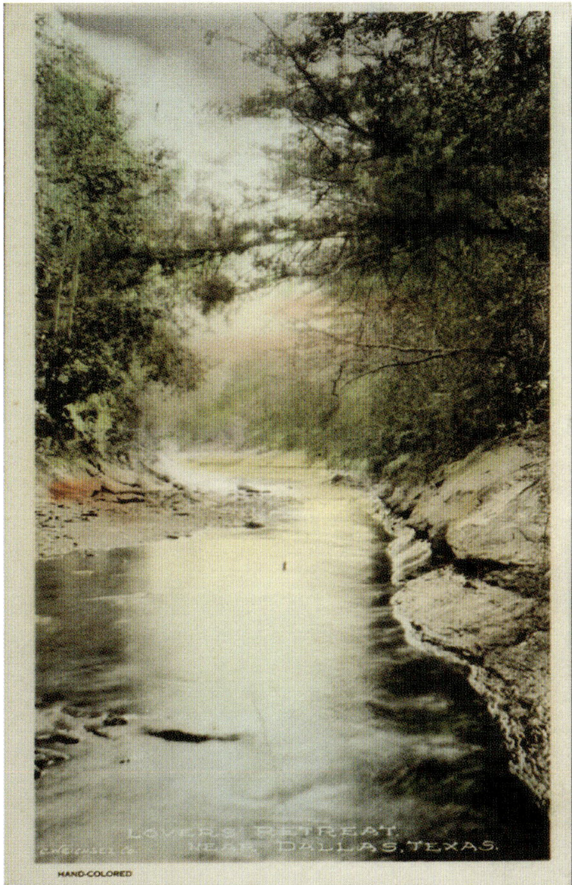

A calming shoreline near Dallas—for lovers.

Circa 1914, $2-4

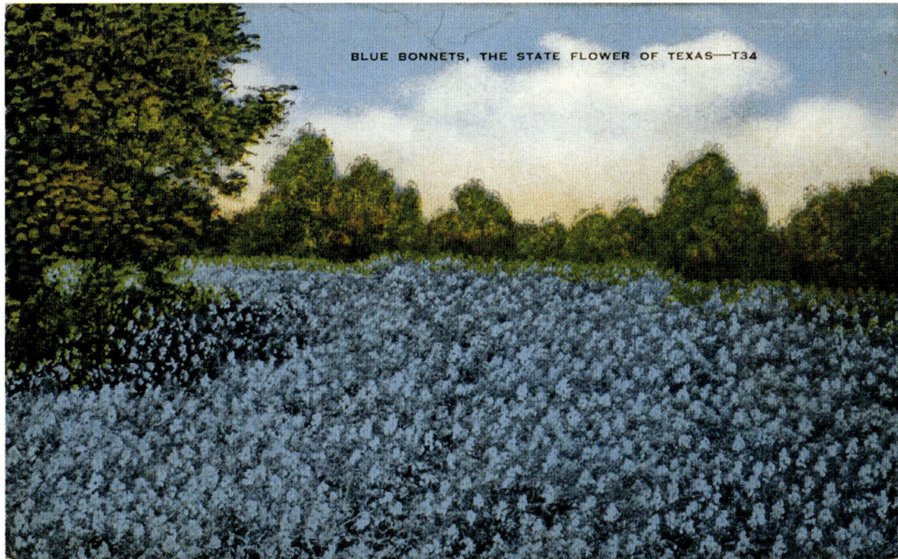

The lovely Blue Bonnet is the official flower for Texas. Seen covering hillsides of residential and park-like neighborhoods, the sky-blue splendor annually attracts both tourists and artists alike.

Circa 1910, $2-4

The West Begins in Dallas, Texas!

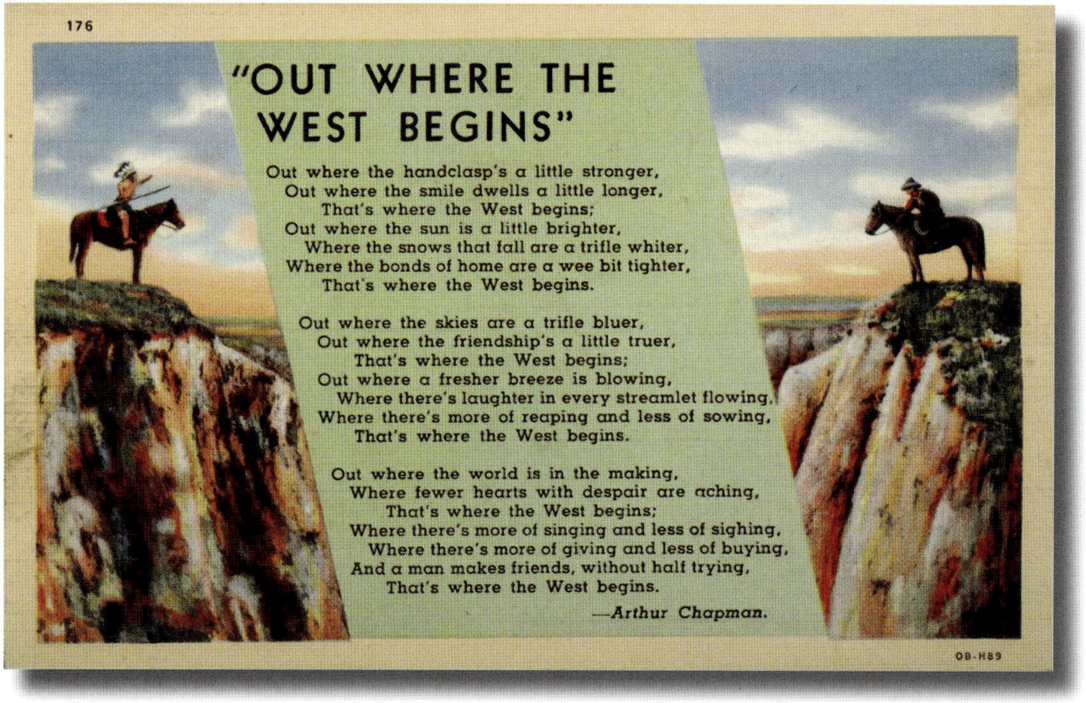

Circa 1940, $2-4
Circa 1914, $2-4

Bibliography and Resources

Anderson, Brian. "1901-1925. 1912: Bridge Over Troubled Water." Dallas Morning News. 03/28/07. http://www.dallasnews.com.

Bluffton University. http://www.bluffton.edu/~sullivanm/texas/dallas/fairpark/hallofstate.html.

City of Lake Dallas. http://www.lakedallas.com.

Dallas Architecture. http://www.dallasarchitecture.info/gulfstates.htm.

Dallas Baptist University (Gaston Avenue Baptist Church). http://www.dbu.edu/.

Dallas City Hall. http://www.dallascityhall.com.

Dallas Convention and Visitors Bureau. http://www.dallascvb.com.

The Dallas Country Club. http://www.thedallascc.org/.

Dallas Historical Society. http://www.dallashistory.org.

The Dallas Library. http://dallaslibrary.org.

Daughters of Charity. http://www.daughtersofcharityfdn.org.

East Dallas Christian Church. http://edcc.org/

Emporis Buildings. http://www.emporis.com.

The Fairmont Hotel—Dallas. http://www.fairmont.com/dallas.

First Baptist Church. http://www.firstdallas.org.

First Methodist Church. http://www.firstchurchdallas.org.

First Presbyterian Church. http://www.presbyterians.org.

The Handbook of Texas Online. http://www.tsha.utexas.edu.

Highland Park Methodist Church. http://www.hpumc.org.

Highland Park Presbyterian Church. http://www.hppc.org.

Historic Fair Park. http://www.watermelon-kid.com.

The Munger Place. http://www.mungerplace.com.

Museum of Nature and Science. http://www.natureand-science.org.

National Register of Historic Places. http://www.nationalregisterofhistoricplaces.com.

Old Oak Cliff Conservation League. http://www.oocl.com.

Southern Methodist University. http://www.smu.edu.

The State Fair of Texas. http://www.bigtex.com.

Southern Methodist University. http://www.smu.edu.

J. D. Tippit. http://www.jdtippit.com.

The Virtual Tourist. http://www.virtualtourist.com.

W. T. Waggoner Estate. http://www.waggonerranch.com.

World Book Encyclopedia. "Dallas." Field Enterprises, Inc. Chicago, IL, 1949.

World Book Encyclopedia. "Texas." Field Enterprises, Inc. Chicago, IL, 1949.

Index